This sweet love story continues ...

for Jayman

One gram of
#happiness
One spoon of
#selfworth

CELEBRATE YOUR SWEET TOOTH

Plant-based recipes using real ingredients as close
to nature intended it to be with low human interference

CHEF CYNTHIA LOUISE

Desserts get a bad rap
sometimes.

As children we can only have
dessert "after you've eaten
your veggies".

They're used as a reward.
As a bribe. They are withheld
as punishment, they are
forbidden and then at birthdays
and Christmases we overindulge.

They also bring back sweet
memories too. In these pages
you'll meet my Dad and his
Anzac Cookies, my Mum and
her Fruit Salad. You'll meet
Rachelle's (Mum's) Pavlova,
Hayley's Brownie and Daina's
Childhood Chocolate Chunks.

This is not justification to
eat desserts all the time.
Just because some of these
recipes contain sweet potato,
dates and berries, doesn't
mean you can eat my (Adults
Only) Chocolate Cupcakes
or my Banoffee Cheesecake
all day, every day.

But I have chosen ingredients
which leave you feeling good.

They nurture your body and its
organs. They won't lift you
up on a refined sugar high and
then dump you afterwards.

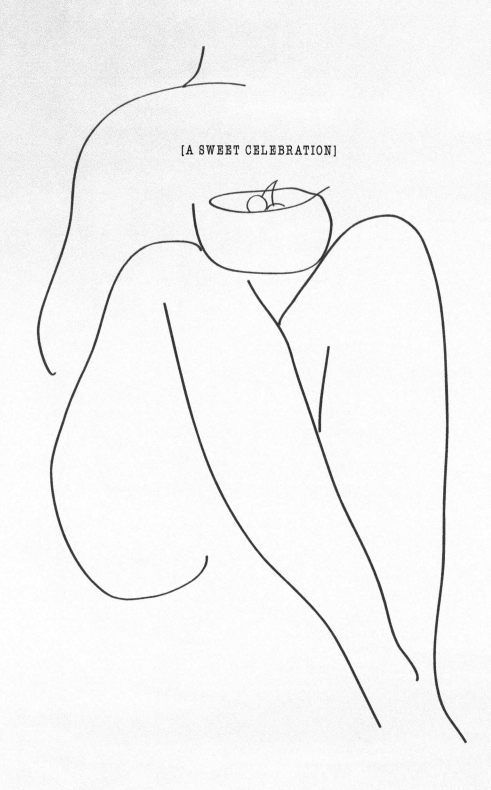

[A SWEET CELEBRATION]

A Sweet Love Letter to My Body

My dear sweet body,

First of all I'm sorry
I have called you fat
I have called you worthless
I have looked in the mirror and
wanted you different.

I have eaten food but tasted guilt
I have looked for joy but swallowed sadness
I have looked for comfort and starved
you instead.

From this day on
I wish every day to be a celebration
To enjoy the miracle that is You: my body
To nourish You with wonderful,
delicious food
To fill You with the sweetness of Life.

And as we sit together quietly,
As my Heart and Mind love you gently
over a plate of Nature's Candy
I will celebrate your sweet tooth naturally.

And every day
In more and more ways

I love you

Chef Cynthia Louise xx

Celebrate your sweet tooth naturally

Banoffee Cheesecake

Contents

Love Letter 6

Introduction 10

A Message from Kat Dawes 15

Recipes 18

Flashtags 260

In the Pantry 264

Equipment 272

Acknowledgements 276

About Chef Cynthia Louise 278

Recipes Index 282

Introduction

Desserts are a connection to childhood reuniting us to our childhood memories.

There will be times when you feel like quitting and buying a packet mix sugar shit storm mud cake. But you should not give up so easily.

I was that kid that barely attended school. Disruptive, loud, and very, very impatient.

Basically, I was every parent's worst nightmare.

I would beg my parents to let me stay at home because I would rather be running around at the back of Dad's workshop climbing mango trees, squatting down to shred coconuts or cook rice on the fire in a rusty old metal pot.

I would loudly chew local food with my mouth open wherever I would find it, and this, to me, was happiness - not shopping for clothes, putting on makeup or buying the next Greatest Hits tape (yes, I'm a child of the 70's).

Today, I choose to spend my time and money on all things related to food.

Whether it's a food adventure in Australia, visiting farmer's markets on islands in Southeast Asia, or establishing a new style of eating in South Africa, my journey so far in this life has been full of passion.

It's also been super freaking painful. But it's made me the person that I am today.

I've survived two open heart surgeries, left the father of my child, raised a beautiful boy, and married my best friend who passed away too soon, before his time.

I've always been a solo businesswoman working for myself. My last shop failed. That was hard.

It was, um, a fish and chip shop on the beach in Tasmania, and let's just say we had a wonderful summer, but no one exactly wants to eat fish and chips on a Tassie beach in winter...

When I returned crying to my parent's place with my tail between my legs and just a mattress on the floor, I cast about in despair for what to do.

Amongst my friends (and thank God for my friends), I was the one that everyone would talk about: **"We're going to Cynthia's for dinner".**

Their advice was "you're a great cook - why don't you become a chef?"

My Dad also encouraged me ("Cynthia, you can do anything you want"), and that's how I found myself knocking on the door of a health retreat begging for a job as an apprentice.

"You're too old," they said.

"I'll do anything," I said.

"You can't be trained," they said.

"I can wash the dishes."

"Alright. You can wash the dishes. And we'll pay you apprentice wages".

And for the princely sum of $6 an hour, I found myself peeling veggies, scrubbing pots, and attending culinary school with 17 year olds.

Not quite the raging success story you imagined.

But maybe you're wrong.

Right then and there I realised as I was cutting veggies, stirring sauces and cracking eggs, I was surrounded by great chefs and Living The Dream.

I was living the dream of becoming a chef, and this was just the first step of many that put me where I am today, with this glorious book in your hands and these glorious words in your mind.

You can do anything you want.

That job taught me a lot.

I was humbled. But I realised that it's not about the money.

It's always about the presence. How you feel. The joy that you create. And the individual moments that make up a life.

It's about shining in from the end result - because I already had the feeling of being a success right from the start.

We are all a sticky bowl of mess

never forget to lick the spoon

The Big Ass Chocolate Cake

The World's Worst Baker

I love being a chef. It's creative, it's dynamic, you make decisions in the moment and you (and your food) can live and die in those moments. It's a glorious organic rush and it turns me on quite frankly.

Cooking I can do. But baking? Make me measure stuff? Time things? Adjust dials and follow procedures?

I need to shake things and stir things and stick my fingers in things and add more things until the magic is right there in the moment.

Bakers are like a careful scientist. They measure. They apportion. They mix. They place. And then they wait…

I have always loved the craftsmanship of a pastry chef, and the art and dedication of their patience. They drift through the kitchen wearing time like an apron and remind me of a superhero - one that never fails or falls as they float through a 16 hour day with their baking superhero powers - flawless in their execution and manipulation of ingredients, technique, skill, scales and temperature.

Pastry chefs are my heroes. And I never thought I had the patience and attention to detail required to bake.

My friend Jon

There are not many men I trust to be straight up with me (besides my son Jayman who is the KING of saying how it is). The very talented Jon Gwyther, however, is someone I can 100% rely on to tell me how it is (sometimes whether I ask him or not!).

It's why we have formed such a mateship over the years, because if you know anything about me, you know I say it how it is.

He's a fellow creative, an incredible director and cinematographer and his beautiful work graces the backcover of this book (thanks mate).

One day as we were sampling some of the creations in this book, Jon faced me down with his stern and caring eyes. I took a moment to swallow and breath as I told myself "here we go, hold on to your ego Cynthia".

In a clear and focussed voice he said "You are not the world's worst baker mate. And you will not be calling this book that or have it plastered over the front cover. These desserts I've been sampling and Gun Gun's food photography is quality, real quality. It's genius and it has class in its favour and most of all it has integrity, just like you my friend".

I looked at him and replied in one simple word. Ok!

If it's one thing

If it's one thing this book is about, it's belief.

My friends believe in me.

My Dad believes in me.

Jon believes in me.

And most importantly. I believe in me.

I believed in me enough to give it a go. And so can you.

Whether you think you're the world's worst baker. Whether you've tried something and failed. Whether you've succeeded at something and then failed (that's kinda even worse). Or whether you're just starting something for the first time, I want you to know this:

I believe in you.

That's why I wrote this book.

Because if you're holding this in your hand there's some creative spark in you that decided "I can cook, and I can bake".

And if you can learn to cook and you can learn to bake, you can learn to do anything.

I learnt to wash dishes. And then I learnt to cook. Now I'm learning to write cookbooks.

I can't wait to see what I'll learn next. And I hope you'll be there with me, celebrating the sweetness of life.

 Chef Cynthia Louise xx

#Celebrate

Chocolate Spread

An Invitation from Kat Dawes

You are invited to dine on one of the most delicious vibrations of all time. A vibration so high it can throw the doors of your heart open and rupture your face into a smile! #Celebrate. A favourite frequency amongst children and other free creatures of your planet, this emotion is most enjoyable, yet ironically, increasingly rare.

As the world tries to trick us into thinking we have less and less things to #celebrate, I invite you to join us and stand firm in your present moment. Represent a sweet vibration, #celebrate, as an ingredient you can use everyday. May you allow it to become your way of BEing.

#celebrate everything in general and nothing in particular, and as you do, I promise you will be delighted by what follows... A continuous and relentless flow of more and more 'reasons' to #celebrate.

Rumour has it... #celebrate is too decadent, too rich, too sublime for feeling all the time. It should be saved for 'special moments' and unleashed at worthy events.

#celebrate is an Endangered Frequency facing extinction from not being felt!

#celebrate needs you! Like electricity looking for an outlet, #celebrate needs an instrumentality to express through.

#celebrate has a high vibrational value, it's not just the party vibe, it can be subtle and sustainable - it is ALWAYS available.

#celebrate this moment and fall in love with where you are.

#celebrate the mango, the plates, the air, your hands. #celebrate you're breathing. #celebrate every moment you can.

#celebrate is not your finalé, #celebrate is where you start.

You don't have a thing to #celebrate?

Can you hear your beating heart?

YOU are the reason to #celebrate - this vibe has chosen you.

Guaranteed if you feel it all the time, it will not lose its shine, it will stabilise and normalise and make for a sweeter life!

Like icing on The Big Ass Chocolate Cake, spread #celebrate evenly over your entire life.

Start where you are, with what you've got - #celebrate a little - and do it a LOT!

Kat Dawes ∞

French Toast

White Chocolate Cake

*The tradition of a birthday remains the same; there is always cake and candles.
Celebrate one's life by lighting a candle; the "light of life"
represents the hope of another year of this life.*

*While we now have an endless list of different types of cakes, this excellent white
chocolate cheesecake is a celebration of how amazing and creative we all are.*

*To be able to make something different and have a feeling of playing with art, then
this cake would have to be my favourite cake (outside of the other favourite ones).*

This must go into the freezer to set, defrost it in the fridge, then you're good to go.

Ingredients

FOR THE BASE

145g oats
60g desiccated coconut
60g sunflower seeds
40g tahini
1 tsp vanilla extract
A pinch of salt
30ml maple syrup
15ml water

FOR THE FILLING

250g cacao butter, melted
300g cashew, soaked
overnight, then rinsed
15ml lemon juice
1 tsp vanilla extract
250ml maple syrup
4-6 chocolate drops
(medicine flower essence)

FOR THE ICING

100gms of melted
dark chocolate

PREP TIME 15 mins
FREEZER-FRIENDLY Yes
R, RSF, V, GF

Method

TO PREPARE THE BASE

Line a round 22cm springform tin with baking paper.

In a food processor, process all of the base ingredients
till fine and sticky. Add more water if needed.

Transfer the base to the tin and press the base firmly
until evenly flat.

TO PREPARE THE FILLING

In a high-speed blender, add all the ingredients
(except for the cacao butter).

Blend on high until creamy and smooth, then add the cacao
butter and blend for a few seconds until well combined.

Transfer the filling to the base and freeze till firm.

Splatter melted chocolate over the frozen cake,
let it defrost then cut and serve.

MAKES 12-16 SLICES

Jam Drop Cookies

What can I say?

These are the classic cookie to pair with a cup of tea when my mates drop by.

Even better if they come straight out of the oven,
just wait 10 minutes for them to cool and serve them hot.

Otherwise, keep them in the fridge in a tight container
and they will last - at least until somebody finds them.

My jam makes the whole situation come together too.
I'm literally going to make another batch after I finish this sentence
- they're that good.

Ingredients

10g whole flax seeds
45ml water
1 tsp baking powder
200g Bob's Red Mill
Gluten Free All-Purpose
Baking Flour
50g desiccated coconut
A pinch of salt
100ml maple syrup
80ml coconut oil
1/2 tsp cinnamon powder
1/2 tsp vanilla extract
100g homemade jam
50ml #ACCEPTANCE

Method

Mix the flax seeds and water and set aside for 5-8 minutes.

Preheat your oven to 170C / 340F.

Add all the ingredients to a bowl and with a wooden spoon mix until well combined.

Using 1 tablespoon as a measurement, scoop the dough and arrange the cookies on a standard baking tray lined with greaseproof paper. Do not crowd the baking tray - been there, done that, didn't work.

Make a small dent in the centre of each cookie.

Fill the dents with some of my homemade jams. (not too much, just a little)

Bake in the preheated oven for 12 minutes.

Leave on a wire rack to cool.

Store in air-tight container in the fridge.

PREP TIME 10-12 mins
BAKING TIME 12 mins
FREEZER-FRIENDLY Yes
C, GF, RSF, NF, V

MAKES 20-25 COOKIES

Chocolate Crackles

Rice Crackles

Remember Chocolate Crackles? Basically cocaine for kids right? Icing sugar, copha (what the hell is copha anyway?), cocoa powder and Rice Bubbles.

I remember feeling high as a kite after my first one - and I also remember wanting MORE before I'd even finished the one I was eating. Talk about addiction.

As a child of the 70s my Mum hardly ever gave us sweets except on birthdays and other celebrations.

Then we would really go to town on all the things we were never normally allowed.

This version of Rice Crackles won't make you high. It will keep your feet firmly on the ground without that crazy high (and the nasty crash afterward). Your kids will thank you too.

Ingredients

150g puffed rice
or amaranth
80g pumpkin seeds,
activated
50g coconut powder
150g dried currants
200g 70% chocolate,
melted
100g dried sour cherries
50g #INSPIRATION

Method

Add all the ingredients to a bowl and mix until well combined.

Transfer the mixture to a square 27.5x18x3cm rectangle tray lined with baking paper.

Spread evenly and press down firmly so that the mixture shapes into a solid base 4cm thick.

Pop into the fridge for 1-2 hours to set.

Slice into chunks of the size you like and enjoy!

PREP TIME 5 mins
FREEZER-FRIENDLY Yes
R, RSF, GF, NF, V

MAKES 12-15 SLICES

Coconut Butter

Coconut Butter

Coconut Butter is expensive. Like over $20 a jar in Australia. And it's one ingredient. Coconut #genius. It's definitely a great butter to have in your pantry. Sometimes I have roasted the coconut till golden brown to get a little more depth of flavour and it was epic. Either way, it's a fantastic ism to have on the shelf. FYI don't put it in the fridge, it turns into a solid.

Ingredients

700g desiccated coconut

Method

Add the coconut to your high-speed blender.

Blend with your high-speed blender using your tamper move the coconut around so the blender can catch all the coconut. This will take 5-6 minutes at high speed.

Transfer to a jar, leaving the lid off till completely cooled down and store in your pantry.

PREP TIME 1 min
FREEZER-FRIENDLY No
R, NF, GF, RSF, V

MAKES 350-400ML JAR

Banana Choc Chip Muffins

I took these on a weekend away with 12 others and they loved them.
Keep em in the fridge because this helps them firm up and then they
become super decadent - just the way I like them.

Ingredients

350g ripe bananas, mashed
100ml maple syrup
300ml coconut milk
50ml coconut oil
100g coconut butter
1 tsp vanilla extract
200g 80% chocolate,
roughly chopped
(you can use chocolate
chips instead)
130g coconut sugar
200g Bob's Red Mill
Gluten Free All-Purpose
Baking Flour
1 1/2 tsp baking powder
20g chia seeds, ground
A pinch of salt
10g #FAITH

Method

Preheat your oven to 170C/340F.

Prepare a cupcake tray with 12 cupcake paper cups
and set them aside.

Mash the bananas, maple syrup, milk, oil, coconut butter,
vanilla extract, and chocolate.

In a separate bowl, combine the coconut sugar, flour,
baking powder, chia and salt.

Fold the two mixtures together and let rest in the bowl
for 10 minutes. Then divide the batter evenly among the
paper cups.

Bake for 30 minutes.

Let the cupcakes cool down before serving

Store in the fridge.

PREP TIME 5-8 mins
BAKING TIME 30 mins
FREEZER-FRIENDLY No
C, RSF, NF, V

MAKES 12 CUPCAKES

Double Choc Chip Cookies

Don't eat them all
they are for the
kids..
Gxx

Double Choc Chip Cookies

I am famous for my cookies (well i think i am) lol.

*I am totally addicted to them and all my friends know that I hunt down
great cookies wherever I can find them.*

*I can tell when a cookie is out of alignment... White sugar, low quality fats, dairy-filled
fake chocolate, the list goes on. I'm a label nazi when it comes to cookies that's for sure.*

*So when I craft a batch of cookies I often don't tell anyone! When someone comes
over and looks in the fridge they'll be all upset that I didn't tell them.*

You want to know why I don't say anything? Because they're That Good!

*While I was making this recipe book I obviously had to make all the desserts
for the photos. After making 6-10 desserts in a day I needed somebody to come
over and eat them. Lucky I have great friends!*

*Unfortunately I got caught out one day because I made these cookies
(along with lots of other desserts) but I didn't put them out to eat at the end of the day!*

*Later on my friends spotted the cookies in the photo of the day and they were
more than a little upset...*

With this recipe you can now make your own.

All I'm saying is, I won't tell anyone if you want to keep them a secret too.

*You deserve a little something just for yourself :)
And don't forget to save some for the kids.*

Ingredients

10g whole flax seeds
45ml water
1 tsp baking powder
200g Bob's Red Mill
Gluten Free All-Purpose
Baking Flour
30g cacao powder
A pinch of salt
100ml maple syrup
80ml coconut oil
50ml plant milk
1/2 tsp vanilla extract
200g chocolate chips
50ml #ACCEPTANCE

Method

Mix the flax seeds and water and set aside for 5-8 minutes.

Preheat your oven to 170C / 340F.

Add all the ingredients to a bowl and with a wooden spoon
mix until well combined.

Using a tablespoon as measurement, scoop the dough and
arrange the cookies on a standard baking tray lined with
greaseproof paper. Do not crowd the baking tray.

Flatten the surface of each cookie.

Bake in the preheated oven for 12 minutes.

Leave on a wire rack to cool.

PREP TIME 10-12 mins
BAKING TIME 12 mins
FREEZER-FRIENDLY Yes
C, GF, RSF, NF, V

MAKES 20-25 COOKIES

Cacao Powder

Cacao Butter

Cacao Paste

Cacao beans

Cacao nibs

Fresh Cacao Pods

Cacao Pods

Growing up in New Guinea, we never really had doors. Life was lived outside, and doors were mainly to keep things in, rather than keep things out.

One of my friends pointed out that my door is always open. People are welcome at my place, and I love that sense of friends dropping by unannounced. They know there is always food in my fridge and a story to tell or hear. And if you're not careful I'll give you a job while you're here.

It reminds me of village life, where life happens outdoors and not on a screen.

In a world where we are quick to guard and only show the best parts of ourselves, where social media creeps in and demands attention like a spoiled teenager, I treasure my raw, human interactions more than anything else.

What's all this got to do with cacao pods you ask?

When my friend The Great Writer Man came over he recognised some cacao pods on my bench and casually asked "so how is chocolate made?" guess what we did?

That's right – we Googled it.

Not.

We absolutely did not Google that shit.

What happened was I grabbed a knife, hacked open one of the pods and I showed him the cacao pods covered in sweet pulp.

We teased out the pods and talked about the fermentation process - how the pods and sweet pulp are placed in wooden barrels covered in banana leaves or hessian and fermented to start liberating the flavour of chocolate.

Then, fermented beans are dried in the sun and from there they are slowly roasted on low heat (or they can be raw) and the husk is removed and the cacao nibs are left.

I pulled out a jar of nibs and we snacked on their dark, earthy flavour while we discussed the way they are crushed by a stone wheel and slowly ground down to form cacao liquor.

There's nothing alcoholic about cacao liquor but we were definitely high on life as I separated some shavings of cacao liquor from a large brown block of pure chocolate.

The cacao liquor is then pressed to liberate more of the fat, creating cacao butter. As I shaved thin slices from a creamy block of cacao butter, we could taste where chocolate's melt-in-your-mouth character comes from.

The 'cake' which is left after the cacao butter is removed is turned into cacao powder, which we spilled across the table and dabbed up with our fingers.

It was a beautiful way to spend an evening with the raw materials of chocolate combined with the raw materials of life: curiosity, adventure and friendship.

How we combine them gives your life its unique flavour.

Adult Only Decadent Chocolate Cupcakes

Ping ping ping! I looked at my phone to see a flurry of messages from Russ my Great Writer Man.

"Chef... Chef!! What the hell? Those Decadent Chocolate Cupcakes you left at my house last night are not for kids. I repeat NOT FOR KIDS!!"

"Right-o mate, right O" I replied. "I know they're good eh?"

"They are insane. Just half a cupcake is more than enough."

"So what shall we call them then??

"(Adults Only) Decadent Chocolate Cupcakes!"

Reader, you have been warned.

Ingredients

180g raw white quinoa,
cooked (cooled)
190g coconut sugar
100g cacao powder
10g baking powder
1/4 tsp salt
40g chia seeds, ground
50ml coconut oil
50ml olive oil
250ml coconut milk
125ml maple syrup

CHOCOLATE FROSTING

1/2 recipe of my chocolate
frosting from the Big Ass
Chocolate Cake
30ml #COURAGE

Method

Preheat your oven to 170C / 340F.

Prepare a cupcake tin and 12 large cupcake paper cups and set aside.

Add all the cupcake ingredients to a food processor and process for about 2 minutes. After 2 minutes let the batter to rest for 10 minutes.

Pour 1/3 cup of the batter into each paper cup.

Bake in the preheated oven for about 25 minutes.

When done, allow the cupcakes to cool down a bit by leaving them in the cupcake tin.

Transfer to a wire rack and put in the fridge to completely cool. They must set in the fridge.

Pipe chocolate frosting on top of the cupcakes when completely cooled down. Put them in the fridge for the icing to set and enjoy!

Store in the fridge – these are not normal fluffly cupcakes.

*make sure that the quinoa is cooled down completely before using. I leave mine in the fridge the night before.

PREP TIME 35 mins
RESTING TIME 10 mins
BAKING TIME 25 mins
FREEZER-FRIENDLY No
C, GF, RSF, NF, V

MAKES 12 CUPCAKES

Not all ovens are made equal…mine is hot and fast, yours might be slow and hot so be prepared to adjust your temperature and please make sure you put baking recipes on the middle shelf not the bottom or the top, the middle!

Hot Cross Buns

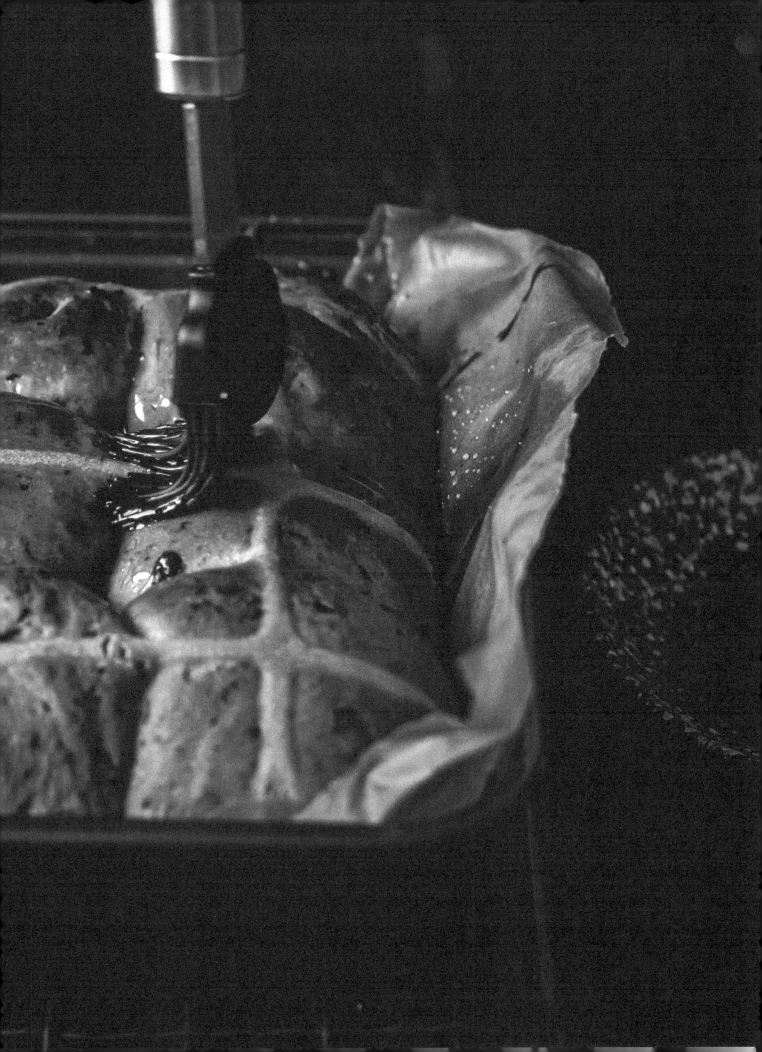

Hot Cross Buns

I'd never come across a Hot Cross Bun until I moved to Australia,
but how glad I was when it finally happened.

Fragrant, delicious bread full of spices and sweet fruit,
these should be eaten all year round if I had my way.
Sliced and toasted with my homemade jam and life is so much more sweeter

Don't wait until Easter to enjoy these.

Ingredients

FOR THE HOT CROSS BUNS

70ml coconut oil
250ml any plant milk, lukewarm
11g baker's yeast
60g coconut sugar
500g white spelt flour
2 tsp chia seeds, ground
2 tsp allspice
2 tsp cinnamon
A pinch of salt
150g currants
10g #GRATITUDE

FOR THE PIPING

80g white spelt flour
A pinch of salt
15ml maple syrup
110ml water

FOR BRUSHING

80ml maple syrup

PREP TIME 10-15 mins
PROVING TIME 55 mins
BAKING TIME 12-15 mins
FREEZER-FRIENDLY Yes
C, RSF, NF, V

Method

TO PREPARE THE HOT CROSS BUNS

Line a square 20.8cm x 20.8cm x 4.5cm baking tin with greaseproof paper and set aside.

Add the coconut oil, milk (warm), yeast, sugar, and flour to your dough mixer.*

Mix for a few seconds and then add the chia, spices, salt, and currants.

Knead the dough for at least 8-10 minutes.

Place the dough into an oiled bowl, cover with a tea towel and keep it in a warm place for 30 minutes until doubled in size.

Knock down the dough and divide it into 8-12 pieces.

Roll the pieces into balls and place them close together on the prepared baking tray.

Give the buns 25 more minutes for proving.

*If you don't have an electric mixer with a dough hook, mix together the ingredients, tip out onto your working surface and knead the dough.

Preheat your oven to 200C / 390F.

TO PREPARE THE PIPING

Mix the ingredients until well combined. You're after a thick paste, so if you need a little more flour or water than add it.

Transfer the mixture to a piping bag and pipe a cross on the top of each bun.

Bake the buns in the preheated oven for 15-20 minutes.

When done, remove from the oven and brush with the maple syrup.

Allow to cool slightly and then pull apart and eat.

MAKES 8-12 BUNS

Mixed Berry Crumble

This dish is dedicated to all the wonderful Grandmas and Mums out there who have made and served crumble for their families and friends.

Crumble is pure love. You can't go wrong with a crumble, and this is no exception.

Ingredients

FOR THE BERRY MIX

1kg frozen berries of your choice
100ml maple syrup
1 1/2 tsp cornflour
15ml water
10g #COMFORT

FOR THE CRUMBLE

140g white spelt flour
55g coconut sugar
50g oats
A pinch of salt
60ml coconut oil, frozen and broken into pieces
60ml ice water

Method

TO PREPARE THE BERRY MIX

Add the berries to a pot and bring to the boil.

Pour in the maple syrup, reduce the heat to a low simmer and cook for 20 minutes until the berry mixture reduces in volume.

In a small bowl, whisk together the cornflour and water, stir into the berries and cook for one more minute.

Turn off the heat and transfer the berry mixture into a round 30cm baking dish or cast iron pan and set aside.

TO PREPARE THE CRUMBLE

Preheat your oven at 160C / 320F.

Add the flour, sugar, oats, and salt to your food processor and pulse to combine.

Add the frozen coconut oil pieces and pulse again until the mixture becomes crumbly.

Pour in the ice water and pulse again. The mixture should resemble dough and you'll know it's ready once you can easily roll it into a ball.

Grab a handful of the dough, gently squeeze and sprinkle evenly over the berries until they are fully covered.

Bake in the preheated oven for 30 minutes or until the crumble is golden brown.

Once done, leave to rest and cool down a bit before serving. I love it served with coconut yogurt.

Use any leftover crumble in the Almond Berry Cake recipe.

PREP TIME 5 mins
COOKING TIME 25 mins
BAKING TIME 30 mins
FREEZER-FRIENDLY Yes
C, RSF, NF, V

SERVES 6-8

Maple syrup is my favourite sweetner

Blue Bounty

A Blue Bounty? Why not!

*My friend Kittea introduced me to butterfly pea flower powder.
She's an alchemist. A libationist. A purveyor of fine cocktails
and the creatrix of exceptional elixirs.*

Put simply, she's an epicurean genius, and I'm so glad she's in my life.

*This was my first exploration into the majesty of natural blue colouring
and as a result, these Blue Bounties stand out on any plate or dish.
Oh, and they taste magnificent.*

Ingredients

170g desiccated coconut
55g almond meal
60ml maple syrup
60ml coconut oil
60ml coconut cream
15ml vanilla extract
A pinch of salt
1-2 tsp butterfly pea flower
powder (the colour will
depend on the amount
of powder you use)

FOR COATING

200g 80% dark chocolate,
for coating
30ml #TRUST

Method

Line a square 27.5x18x3cm rectangle tray with baking paper.

Add all the bounty ingredients to your food processor and blend until well combined.

Transfer to the prepared tray and press to spread evenly and shape the mixture into a solid layer.

Cut the bounty layer into bars or squares and freeze.

Remove from the freezer and melt the chocolate and coat each bounty piece.

Arrange your bounty bars onto the tray and return them to the freezer for 15 more minutes.

PREP TIME 5 mins
FREEZER-FRIENDLY Yes
R, RSF, GF, V

MAKES 8-12

The Original Tahini Balls

*I owe this recipe to Yolande, an incredible cook in her 60s
who took me under her wing way back in 2007.*

*She was a master of throwing things together as we created dishes designed to restore
people's health and vitality at the health retreat where we worked.*

*I have memories of being an eager apprentice chef with Yolande, studying what she did
so as not to waste a thing. Every scrap could be turned into something amazing,
and any stuff-up was just a stepping stone to something even more delicious.*

*She found a use for everything – including me
– and I remember her licking her fingers proudly on many an occasion.*

These are the Original Tahini Balls – in honour of you Yolande.

Ingredients

2/3 C ~~150g~~ raw almonds
1/2 C 100g mixed dried fruits of your choice
1/2 cup white tahini
1/2 C 120ml maple syrup
1 C 80g desiccated coconut

FOR COATING

100g desiccated coconut,
10g #CONTENTMENT

Method

Add all the ingredients to your food processor and blend until completely combined and sticky.

Wet your hands and shape the mixture into small balls.

Toast 100g of desiccated coconut for coating the balls.

Place your tahini balls in an air-tight container and store in the fridge for up to 8 days.

PREP TIME 10 mins
FREEZER-FRIENDLY Yes
R, RSF, GF, V

MAKES 20 BALLS

Chocolate Snaps

Hello. My name is Cynthia Louise and I am addicted to biscuits and cookies.

These little glories will disappear as fast as you can make them.
But a word of warning: store them in an airtight container in the fridge or they
may fall apart. There's not much holding them together except for the #easeandflow.

If you want to be extra chocolate cheeky, put some of my Chocolate Spread
on them and make a biscuit sandwich. Guaranteed next level indulgence.

Ingredients

200g white spelt flour
100g coconut sugar
30g cacao powder
A pinch of salt
160 ml coconut oil
20ml #EASE & FLOW

Method

Preheat your oven at 150C / 300F.

Line a standard baking tray with baking paper and set aside.

Add all the ingredients to your food processor and pulse until combined. If needed, stop a couple of times to scrape the sides.

Place the dough between two sheets of baking paper and roll it out until it's 1/2 cm (0.2 in) thick.

Use a round cookie cutter to cut the dough into biscuits. (the dough is wet so be careful)

Roll bits of offcuts of the dough again and cut it into biscuits until all the dough is used.

Carefully arrange the biscuits on the baking tray and bake for 25 minutes.

When done, leave the biscuits to cool down before serving. And make sure you store them in the fridge.

PREP TIME 5 mins
BAKING TIME 25 mins
FREEZER-FRIENDLY No
C, RSF, NF, V

MAKES 10-12 BISCUITS

Ice Pops

Ice Pops

Never buy nasty store-bought ice pops. Instead, you're going to look at all the random bits of fruit in the bottom of your fridge with a gleam in your eye and a cunning plan...

Here's the trick: in a high-speed blender, blend everything until smooth. Taste each mix and see if you need some maple syrup to bring it home.

Then squeeze lime adding just a little at a time. Keep tasting it and as you do, you'll start learning how to balance the flavours.

Lastly, add a pinch of salt and when you can taste the deliciousness, transfer to your moulds and freeze them overnight.

A healthy, guilt-free ice pop for kids and adults alike.

Ingredients

RASPBERRY POPS

1 cup frozen raspberries

1 banana, peeled and chopped into chunks

Maple syrup, as much as you like

A pinch of salt

DRAGON FRUIT RASPBERRY POPS

1 cup frozen raspberries

1 dragon fruit, peeled and roughly chopped

A splash of lime juice

Maple syrup, as much as you like

A pinch of salt

YELLOW POPS

1-2 mangoes, peeled and roughly chopped (discard the seed)

1 super ripe sweet pineapple, peeled, cored and roughly chopped

Maple syrup, as much as you like

A handful of fresh mint leaves

A pinch of salt

REFRESHING PASSION FRUIT POPS

1 orange, peeled and quartered

6-10 passion fruit, pulp only

A splash of lime juice

Maple syrup, as much as you like

A pinch of salt

Method

Add the flavour combos of your choice to a high-speed blender and blend until smooth.

Taste and add more maple syrup if needed.

Transfer the mixture to your moulds and insert popsicles sticks and freeze.

Each flavour is a blissful pop on its own.

PREP TIME 5 mins
FREEZER-FRIENDLY Yes
R, RSF, GF, NF, V

MAKES 2-3 POPS PER FLAVOUR COMBO

Yellow Ice Pop

Raspberry Ice Pop

Dragon fruit Raspberry Ice Pop

Passionfruit Ice Pop

Chewy Bars

This is good all on its own but I tell you what,
cover it in my crack chocolate sauce and the whole thing goes Next Level.

I dare you.

Ingredients

50g coconut flakes
40g pumpkin seeds
40g sunflower seeds
40g black sesame seeds
40g white sesame seeds
25g chia seeds
120g dried currants
1 tsp cinnamon powder
10ml vanilla extract
30ml coconut oil, melted
120ml maple syrup
30g oats
A pinch of salt
20g #JOY

Method

Preheat your oven to 160C / 320F.

Add the ingredients to a food processor and process for 30 seconds.

Transfer the mixture to a square 27.5x18x3cm rectangle tray lined with baking paper.

Place another sheet of baking paper on top of the mixture and press really hard with the tray of the same size (or using a spatula).

Bake in the preheated oven for 15-20 minutes.

When done, allow to cool, then slice into bars and serve.

PREP TIME 8 mins
BAKING TIME 15-20 mins
FREEZER FRIENDLY YES
C, RSF, NF, GF, V

MAKES 12-15 BARS

Truffle Protein Balls

I have to say, these are good. Really good.

The more I processed them the more they turned into a sticky fine dough.
Rolled in coconut and stored in the fridge in a sealed container they are
the sweetest sweeties that keep me on my toes when looking for a treat to snack on.
These are addictive #justsayin

Ingredients

80g cacao paste, chopped
90g almond meal
60g hemp seeds
150g desiccated coconut
70g dried raisins
40g coconut sugar
A pinch of salt
1/4 cup black tahini
30ml water
Desiccated coconut,
for coating
Cacao powder, for coating
50ml #LOVE

Method

Add all the ingredients except black tahini and water to your food processor.

Pulse until all the ingredients are chopped super fine.

Taste and add more sweetener if needed.

Add in the black tahini and start processing while adding water a bit at a time. Add just enough water to keep the ingredients to stick together. (you are after a fine sticky mixture)

Roll the mixture into balls of equal size.

Coat the balls with desiccated coconut and some with cacao powder, enjoy!

PREP TIME 10 mins
FREEZER-FRIENDLY Yes
R, RSF, GF, V

MAKES 22-25 BALLS

This is how you celebrate
your sweet tooth naturally

Chocolate Spread

The raw materials of life: curiosity, adventure and friendship.
How we combine them gives your life its unique flavour.

Dates

Dates are the crown jewel of the Middle East.
A symbol of abundance, prosperity and
hospitality, these sticky, sweet delights are
considered the fruit of heaven and are a
precious ingredient in any dish or dessert.

Dates are a whole food.

The associated fibre and nutrients which
accompany their delicious sweetness prevent
blood sugar from spiking.

Your body knows exactly what to do with this
natural gift. It's the taste of heaven on earth,
and it's here for you to enjoy.

In these recipes, I use dried dates instead
of the fresh, luscious medjool dates.

The only reason is because
I can't get them here!

If you're lucky to have access to fresh
dates then let me know how it goes.
Or use dried dates just the way I do.

Either way you're getting the sweetness
of nature just the way it's intended.

Sticky Date Pudding

Eating this incredibly sweet situation and not looking down on yourself afterwards but gently whispering, I love you.

Sticky Date Pudding

Surround yourself with good friends, I say.

*This sticky date pudding would be nowhere near as epic without a
bit of mentoring (and tough love) from my friend Jon Gwyther.*

*An incredible artist in his own right, he's shot films and photos across the world,
and here he is in my kitchen chowing down my sticky date pud.*

*But as I said - surround yourself with good friends. They all had a hand in these desserts
and I'm grateful for their feedback – it's a million times better than any Google search,
and I will choose their opinion over the internet any time of day.*

*So here's the upgraded version of the classic sticky date pudding.
Let me know how much you love it.*

Ingredients

FOR THE PUDDING

200g dried dates
280ml coconut oil, melted
237ml water
25g chia seeds, ground
2 tsp baking soda
1 1/2 tsp baking powder
133g coconut sugar
1 tsp vanilla extract
A pinch of salt
180g white spelt flour

FOR THE SAUCE

400ml any plant milk
140g dried dates
60g coconut sugar
1 tsp vanilla extract
8 drops of butterscotch
essence, I used Wild
Medicine Flower Essence
A pinch of salt
10ml #SELFWORTH

Method

TO PREPARE THE PUDDING

Preheat the oven to 160C / 320F.

Grease 5 large ramekin cups with coconut oil, dust them
with flour and set aside.

Add everything except the spelt flour to a blender and
blend to combine but still leave a little texture.

Transfer the mixture to a bowl, add the flour and
then combine.

Divide the mixture among the prepared ramekin cups
leaving 2cm from the top.

Place the cups into a large baking pan and fill the pan with
hot water to reach halfway up the sides of the cups.

Bake in the preheated oven for 30-40 minutes.

TO PREPARE THE SAUCE

Add the ingredients to a high-speed blender and blend until
smooth and creamy.

Transfer to a medium-sized pot and bring it to a low simmer,
stirring constantly over medium heat.

When it begins to boil, remove the pot from the heat.

When the puddings are baked, remove them from the oven
and allow to cool slightly.

Run a knife around the edges of the cups and tip the
puddings onto a plate.

Pour the sauce over the puddings and serve.

PREP TIME 10-15 mins
BAKING TIME 40 mins
FREEZER FRIENDLY No
C, RSF, NF, V

MAKES 5 PUDDINGS

White Chocolate
& Hazelnut Cookies

So you need to be sensible with these little bad boys ok.
There are two things you need to know before you go in.

Number one: don't over mix the mix. A slight folding is all you need.

Number two: don't eat them just out of the oven. You will burn your mouth #fact.

Get those two things right and everything else in life will make sense.

Ingredients

200g white spelt flour
1 tsp baking soda
180g white chocolate, cut
into chunks
100g roasted hazelnuts
A pinch of salt
50ml maple syrup
50ml coconut oil
1/2 tsp vanilla extract
100ml plant milk of
your choice
15ml apple cider vinegar
100ml #LETTINGGO

Method

Preheat your oven at 160C / 320F.

Line a standard baking tray with unbleached baking paper and set it aside.

Mix together the dry ingredients and set the mixture aside.

In a separate bowl, whisk together the wet ingredients.

Gently fold the two mixtures together till combine, DO NOT over mix.

Using an ice cream scoop, scoop the cookie dough onto the prepared tray.

Bake in the preheated oven for 15 minutes.

Let the cookies rest for a bit before enjoying them.

PREP TIME 5 mins
BAKING TIME 15 mins
FREEZER-FRIENDLY No
C, RSF, V

MAKES 16 COOKIES

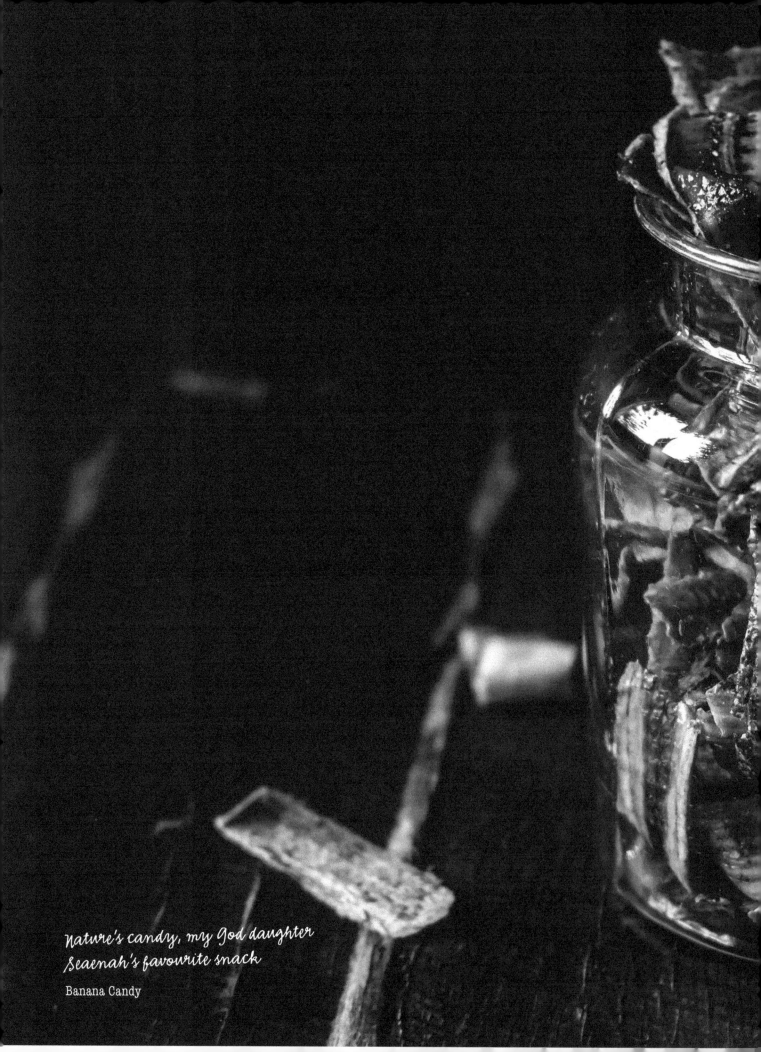

Nature's candy, my God daughter
Seaenah's favourite snack

Banana Candy

Banana Candy

*These EPIC dried bananas are pimped up with a splattering of
coconut sugar and a sprinkle of cinnamon. You might be thinking "why"
add sugar to already sweet bananas? Well, it was a genius move to be honest
– created by my good friend Rachelle many years ago.*

*How she came up with the idea to sprinkle on these isms was something I questioned
at the time, but now I can't imagine dried bananas any other way.*

*So this very fragrant and sweet recipe is brought to you today as a gift from
Rachelle (who by the way never cooks anything ever and thinks kitchens are just
storage spaces for plates and glasses).*

*You can really celebrate your sweet tooth naturally with
these babies and you will never reach for the lolly jar again.*

Ingredients

5kg bananas*
1/2 tsp coconut sugar,
on each slice
cinnamon, sprinkle
10g #FUN

*5kg was enough to
fill my 9-tray Excalibur
dehydrator.

Method

Slice the bananas lengthwise and make sure that all slices
are the same thickness. I got around 5 slices per banana.

Arrange the slices in a single layer on your dehydrator
mesh sheets.

Sprinkle with coconut sugar and sprinkle cinnamon.

Turn on your dehydrator to around 42C / 107F and let the
banana slices transform into candies. It will take around 8
to 10 hours.

When done, remove the banana slices from the dehydrator
tray and leave to cool.

Store in an airtight container.

PREP TIME 10 mins
TIME TO DEHYDRATE 8-10 hours
FREEZER-FRIENDLY No
R, RSF, NF, GF, V

MAKES 3.5-4KG

Almond and Orange Cake

Pouring orange glaze over the top of this cake straight out of the oven is next level.

Orange glaze kinda looks like this: juice of 2 oranges and add a little maple syrup (as sweet as you want).

Simmer it gently till it cooks to a syrup type consistency, then pour this over the hot cake, let it cool completely and store in the fridge till you're ready.

The longer it's in the fridge the firmer it becomes.

Normally this cake would have 6-8 eggs, which also gives it a yellow colour. If you really want that shade of yellow just add more turmeric.

Ingredients

2 oranges, whole
7-9L water
30g chia seeds, ground
200ml maple syrup
270g almond meal
3 tsp baking powder
1 tsp turmeric powder, for colour
1 1/2 tsp green cardamom seeds
3-4 drops Young Living Orange Essential Oil
50ml #RESPECT

Method

Line a round 22x4cm tin with baking paper and set it aside.

Fill a pot with water, add the oranges making sure there is enough water so the oranges are covered and boil them for 30-45 minutes. Once done, discard the water.

Boil the oranges again in clean water for another 45 minutes. When done, discard the water.

Repeat the same process again, discard the water and set the oranges aside to cool. (All up, three times boiled).

Preheat your oven to 170C / 320F.

When the oranges are cooled, add them to your food processor, blend and transfer to a bowl.

In a large bowl, whisk the chia seeds, oranges, essential oil and maple syrup.

In a separate bowl, mix together the almond meal, baking powder, turmeric powder, and cardamom.

Add the dry mix to the wet and mix gently to combine.

Pour the mixture into the prepared baking tin and let it sit for 10 minutes then bake for an hour.

Once cooked, allow to cool in the tin completely and store in the fridge so it will firm up. (This cake must be kept in the fridge)

Enjoy!

PREP TIME 2h 10 mins
BAKING TIME 1h
FREEZER-FRIENDLY Yes
C, RSF, GF, V

MAKES 15 SLICES

I've come up with this little situation of glory.

Hayley's Brownie

Hayley's Brownie

This is the story of a permaculturist named Hayley, a chef, and a dream to create the perfect plant-based brownie.

Years have passed, along with them have come countless messages from Hayley

- *Eating some random brownie or in a cafe somewhere in the world and telling me I could make a better one*

- *Watching Instagram TV cooking shows in the middle of the night and pinging me awake with requests for a plant-based brownie*

- *Cooking on her tiny portable oven in the bush on her land and demanding I create a recipe she can cook at home...*

If I didn't love her so much it would border on harassment. But I love her dearly. And now it's time to close a chapter.

This is the plant-based brownie for the brownie connoisseur. It's for every hippy cooking out of a tiny oven in their van or on their land. And it's for every gourmet chef that wants to surprise and delight.

It's good for you too. So go get it.

Hayley's Brownie.

Years in the making, and now finally captured in this book for you to enjoy.

Ingredients

250g cacao paste, finely chopped
250g coconut sugar
250g almond meal
3 tsp baking powder
150ml coconut oil
300ml coconut milk
70g chia seeds, ground
10g #HAYLEYSPOSITIVITY

Method

Preheat your oven to 160C / 320F.

Line a square 27.5x18x3cm rectangle tray with baking paper.

Combine the dry ingredients and set aside.

Mix the wet ingredients and add them to the dry mix.

Mix well and pour the batter into the lined tray.

Let the batter sit in the tray for 10 min so the chia soaks up the moisture.

Bake in the preheated oven for 45 minutes.

Allow to cool completely in the tin and keep in the fridge to firm up.

Cut into small square pieces and serve.

PREP TIME 5 minutes
BAKING TIME 45-50 minutes
FREEZER FRIENDLY Yes
C, RSF, GF, V

MAKES 15-20 SQUARES

Black Salted Caramel Cheescake

*Nothing makes me happier than this little salty, cheesey,
creamy number like this incredible yet simple cheese cake.*

*Freezes well #winning and has the taste of caramel
from the medicine flower essences (google them).*

*The black salt was a random gift someone gave to me years ago.
It sat on my kitchen studio shelf in all its black glory.
Blakened by charcoal and bottled by humans. Until one day I decided to use it.*

*This is one of the many recipes that made it into my online masterclass
conveniently called Celebrate Your Sweet Tooth Naturally.
So many of my students make this and can't believe how decadent it is.*

When life gives you black salt I turn it into a salted caramel cheesecake.

Ingredients

FOR THE BASE

40g sunflower seeds, raw
40g pumpkin seeds, raw
100g shredded coconut
50g oats
100g dried dates
1 tsp vanilla extract
1/4 tsp salt
15ml water

FOR THE FILLING

250g cashews, soaked in
4 cups of water for at least
8-12 hours and rinsed well
120ml maple syrup
10 drops of caramel
essence, I used Medicine
Flower Essences
1/2 tsp salt
150g solid cacao butter,
melted
Black charcoal salt for
topping

Method

TO PREPARE THE BASE

Line a round, 24cm x 3.5cm tart tin with greaseproof paper and set aside.

Add the ingredients to a food processor.

Process until well combined and sticky.

Transfer the mixture to the prepared tart tin.

Press down to distribute evenly.

Set aside in the fridge.

TO PREPARE THE FILLING

Add all ingredients (except the butter and black charcoal salt) to your blender.

Blend until completely smooth and creamy.

Add the cacao butter and blend for 10 more seconds.

Pour the filling over the base.

Sprinkle with the black charcoal salt.

Freeze for 40 minutes before serving.

PREP TIME Soaking will take 8-12
hours, the rest is minutes
FREEZER-FRIENDLY Yes
R, RSF, GF, V

MAKES 12-18 SLICES

Muesli Bars

*I love muesli bars, but for some reason I have always bought them
and never thought to make them.*

Well, that's all changed now.

*Today was a great day as I made two batches of these beauties.
The first batch was over-processed. There was not a lot of texture
but it had a great crunch and held together well.*

The next batch is pictured here. Loads of texture and crunch and also held well.

Ahh, perfection.

Make sure you store it in the fridge and all will be well.

Ingredients

150g raw almonds
100g raw walnuts
130g sultanas
25g chia seeds, ground
80g oats
1/2 tsp cinnamon powder
75ml maple syrup
55ml coconut oil, melted
70g almond butter
A pinch of salt
50g #PEACE

Method

Preheat your oven to 130C / 266F.

Add almonds, walnuts, and sultanas to your food processor
and pulse 10 times.

Add the chia, oats, and cinnamon powder and pulse again but
don't overmix.

Transfer to a large bowl and set aside.

In a small pot, add the maple syrup, coconut oil, almond
butter, and salt and heat on low until melted and combined.

Add to the dry mixture and stir to combine.

Transfer to a 27.5x18x3cm rectangle tray lined with
baking paper.

Distribute the mixture evenly, place a sheet of baking paper
on top of the mixture and press hard with another tin of the
same size.

Make the bar lines (otherwise, it will be hard to slice into
bars later) and then bake for 25 minutes.

Leave to cool a bit, slice into bars and then allow to cool
completely.

Store in the fridge for up to 2 weeks
(good luck with that LOL ;))

PREP TIME 10 mins
BAKING TIME 25 mins
FREEZER-FRIENDLY Yes
C, RSF, V

MAKES 9 BARS

Chef Travis's Compote

Eating sweets and feeling on top of the world during and after eating one of my desserts

Chef Travis's Compote

*Chef Travis. My friend. My mentor. My hero. And maybe even my crush.
You're so damn talented it's a turn on mate. This one's for you.*

*I remember what a joy it was when we would cook in my old studio.
I've made many a compote in my time but on this particular day you
opened my mind up to your process and it blew me away.*

*Left to my own devices I would just chuck all the ingredients in a pot and walk away,
but oh no, that's not the way. You taught me to simmer a little, then add the rest,
and pay careful attention until you get perfection.*

*It's not often I meet such a caring, sharing, highly experienced chef like
Chef Travis. This recipe is my tribute to his love and his care.*

Ingredients

350ml water
1 cinnamon stick
1 vanilla pod
3 slivers of fresh ginger,
unpeeled
30g coconut sugar
2 lemon strips, zested
5 dried figs, whole
2 green apples,
peeled, cored and
cut into 6 wedges
100g #INSPIRATION

Method

Combine the first 6 ingredients in a medium-sized pot and bring to the boil.

Turn down the heat to a simmer, add the figs and cook for 10 minutes.

Add the apple wedges, put the lid on and simmer for 10 more minutes.

The compote is done once the apples are soft to the touch but not too soft to fall apart and the liquid has reduced to a syrup.

Serve the compote with ice cream, breakfast pancakes, or muesli.

PREP TIME 10 mins
COOKING TIME 20-35 mins
FREEZER-FRIENDLY No
C, RSF, GF, NF, V

SERVES 4-6

Breakfast Carrot Cake

Back in the day, I would demo this in fasting retreats to show the audience that here is a way to have, eat, and create a new style of carrot cake.

The recipe feels like you could have it for breakfast, dessert or even a snack. It's light, delicious and Oh My Lord that icing! Finger-licking goodness right there in that white gold.

I cut this cake into bite-size pieces and pop them into the freezer so they're ready for whenever.

Ingredients

FOR THE CAKE

400g carrots, unpeeled and grated
300g fresh pineapple, chopped roughly
150g desiccated or shredded coconut
10g cinnamon powder
10g freshly grated ginger
1 tsp turmeric powder
250g almonds, soaked overnight in 500ml water, rinsed and drained
100g dried dates
80g currants
15g psyllium husk
50g hemp hearts
15g chia seeds, ground
60ml maple syrup
A pinch of salt

TANGY CREAMY ICING

300ml Kara coconut cream
10g savoury yeast
45ml lemon juice
150g raw cashew nuts, soaked overnight in 500ml water, rinsed and drained
200g white chocolate, melted
10ml #JOY

PREP TIME 8 mins
UNCOOKING TIME 30 mins
FREEZER-FRIENDLY Yes
R, RSF, GF, V

Method

TO PREPARE THE CAKE

Add all the ingredients to your food processor and process until well combined. If needed, work in batches.

Don't overmix, the base should have a bit of texture (it's not a smoothie).

Transfer the mixture to a square 27.5x18x3cm rectangle tray lined with baking paper.

Press down firmly to shape the mixture into an even layer.

Keep in the fridge to firm up while preparing the icing.

TO PREPARE THE ICING

Add all the ingredients except the chocolate to your blender and blend until creamy and smooth.

Pour in the melted chocolate and blend for 5 more seconds.

Keep in the fridge for about 30 minutes or so to firm up a bit so it's easier to spread.

When ready, spread over the cake.

Allow the cake to rest in the fridge before serving.

MAKES 16-18 SLICES

Choc Chip Cookies

Mine... All mineeeeeee...

What can I say? The more chocolate the better.
I have actually added the entire mixture to a cast iron
frying pan (a small one) and made a BIG ass cookie.
I ate the entire cookie. Took a few days but damn, it was great!

Ingredients

30ml coconut oil, melted
200g coconut sugar
1/2 tsp cinnamon powder
60ml any plant-based milk
of your choice
1 tsp baking powder
1 tsp baking soda
15ml apple cider vinegar
300g chocolate chips
A pinch of salt
200g white spelt
flour, sifted
100g #GRATITUDE

Method

Preheat your oven to 160C / 320F.

Whisk together the oil, sugar, cinnamon, and milk.

Add the baking powder, baking soda, and vinegar and combine until it starts to bubble.

Stir in the chocolate chips and salt and then gently fold in the flour. Don't overmix the batter.

Using an ice cream scoop, scoop the batter onto a standard baking tray lined with baking paper.

Gently push down the scooped cookies to flatten them a bit.

Bake in the preheated oven for 15 minutes.

Allow to cool down before serving.

PREP TIME 10 mins
BAKING TIME 15 mins
FREEZER-FRIENDLY Yes
C, RSF, NF, V

MAKES 18-22 COOKIES

*My Raw White Chocolate Cake about
to go into the fridge to unbake*

Chocolate Truffle Balls

Warning: These Chocolate Truffle Balls are epic, BUT they don't taste like Ferrero Rochers (they just look like them OK).

They are actually the result of a slice recipe I was making which ahem didn't turn out quite right.

I was left with a heap of chocolatey goodness which I decided to roll into little balls - Chocolate Truffle Balls to be precise.

So you may have some explaining to do if you present them like this.

Or you can just enjoy them for their chocolatey truffley deliciousness and decide you'll never need a Ferrero Rocher again.

Just don't tell anybody that they're mainly made of vegetables! Something this sinfully good can actually be good for you too - but let's keep it our little secret.

Ingredients

FOR THE TRUFFLE BALLS

250g sweet potato, baked with skin on

150g beetroot, peeled, grated (squeeze the juice out as much as you can)

200g almond butter or any seed/nut butter

100g Bob's Red Mill Coconut Flour

225ml maple syrup

100g cacao powder

20g chia seeds, ground

1 tsp vanilla extract

A pinch of Salt

10g #GRATITUDE

FOR THE COATING

Chocolate chips, melted. As much as you need.
Crushed nuts, (I used roasted hazelnuts)

Method

Peel the baked potato add to your blender along with the remaining ingredients.

Blend until combined and mixed well.

Transfer to the fridge set overnight.

Once firmed up, roll the mixture into small balls.

Coat them with chocolate or crushed nuts.

PREP TIME 15-20 minutes
SETTING TIME overnight
FREEZER FRIENDLY Yes
C, RSF, GF

MAKES 30-50 BALLS

Almond Berry Cake

One way to use the berry crumble leftovers was in this cake. I have to say it was an epic upcycle. All I did was place what was left of the crumble into the mix. Worked a treat.

Sometimes things work out and sometimes they work out unexpectedly. You be the judge.

All I will say is there's a reason this recipe made it into the book.

Ingredients

100g Bob's Red Mill Gluten Free All-Purpose Baking Flour

200g almond meal

30g chia seeds, ground

A pinch of salt

1 tsp baking soda

10g corn flour

250ml plant milk of your choice

80ml maple syrup

1/2 tsp vanilla extract

80g coconut butter

15ml apple cider vinegar

250g berry crumble from the Mixed Berry Crumble recipe (or a cup of jam)

10g #GRATITUDE

Method

Preheat your oven at 160C / 320F.

Line a round 24cm x 4cm springform tin with baking paper and set aside.

Mix together the dry ingredients and set aside.

Whisk together the wet ingredients in a separate bowl and then stir in the berry crumble leftovers.

Add the wet mixture to the dry one and mix until well combined.

Pour the batter into the baking tin and bake for 40 minutes.

Allow the cake to rest a bit before serving.

PREP TIME 5 mins
BAKING TIME 40 mins
FREEZER-FRIENDLY No
C, RSF, V

SERVES 4-6

Anzac Biscuits

*My dad would buy Anzacs biscuits from the Woolies supermarket.
When he and mum came home he would help her unpack and then
out of the blue would come the delicious smell of baking biscuits.*

*I would get distracted from whatever I was doing and think
"who on earth is baking?"*

*It was my Dad's little trick to crack open the packet of biscuits
and place them on an oven tray with the temperature real low.
They crisped up this way and he liked them crunchy.*

*Baking is always full of memories, and I reckon the smell
reminded him of His childhood because his mum (and my grandma)
would bake Anzac biscuits during the week of Anzac Day.*

Enjoy this version of a great Australian biscuit.

Ingredients

1 tsp baking soda
100g old-fashioned oats
150g white spelt flour
70g coconut sugar
50g desiccated coconut
120ml coconut oil, melted
100ml maple syrup
A pinch of #FORGIVENESS

Method

Preheat your oven to 160C / 320F.

Mix all ingredients in a big bowl, mix well with your hands by squishing the mixture until combined for around 2 minutes (this is a great job for the kids).

Make small balls weighing 40 grams and press them in between your palms to flatten the balls into a biscuit shape and transfer them onto a standard baking tray lined with baking paper.

Bake for 8-12 minutes.

Allow to cool completely on a wire rack before serving.

PREP TIME 5 mins
BAKING TIME 8-12 mins
FREEZER-FRIENDLY No
C, RSF, NF, V

MAKES 15 BISCUITS

Chocolate Orange Truffle Tart

Chocolate Orange Truffle Tart

I declared that this here cake, torte, tart - whatever the pastry chefs call it – this cake, torte, tart Is the best I have ever made.

Rich and decadent. Smooth and lush. Tasty and kind to the organs. I hereby declare this beauty is one of my top 3 desserts in this book.

The texture is perfect. Plus there is no taste of tofu in sight (thank god).

All my non-vegan friends would have made up an excuse to not have a slice if I told them what it was made from. The secret is the silken tofu. It has an incredible texture but none of that plastic tofu taste. And anyway, once your taste buds hit the contrast between the smooth filling and the crunchy biscuit base you'll be sold.

Speaking of tofu, there are some people you can never please, like my brother BJ.

No matter what I cook – even if it's spaghetti or cheese on toast – he'll take a spoonful and say "is that tofu I can taste? Cos it doesn't need it Cyn."

Once at a BBQ he threw some tofu on the grill and served it to me with a wicked smile and said "I found your jandals, Cyn". Me, my brother and tofu have been a running joke for years. But I reckon this cake will finally shut him up. This one's for you BJ!

Ingredients

FOR THE CHOCOLATE CRUST

200g white spelt flour
100g coconut sugar
30g cacao powder
A pinch of salt
160ml coconut oil

FOR THE CHOCOLATE ORANGE FILLING

350g silken or soft tofu, drained
350g 70% chocolate, melted
5-6 drops orange essential oil, I used Young Living brand
10ml #SELFWORTH

PREP TIME 5-8 mins
BAKING TIME 25 mins
FREEZER-FRIENDLY Yes
C, RSF, NF, V

Method

TO PREPARE THE CRUST

Preheat your oven to 160C / 320F.

Add all ingredients to food processor and pulse to combine.

Pause to scrape the sides and then process again until the ingredients come together into a wet dough.

Transfer the dough into a round 24cm x 3.5cm loose bottom tart tin lined with baking paper.

Press and spread evenly and smooth it out to cover the base of your tart tin.

Bake in the preheated oven for 25 minutes. Rotate the tart once during baking.

Once done, allow to rest in the tin for 10 minutes.

TO PREPARE THE FILLING

Add the tofu to the blender and blend until it turns into a thick smooth mixture.

Add the remaining ingredients and blend until creamy and well combined.

Pour the filling over the crust and spread it evenly.

Keep the tart in the fridge until the filling firms up.

MAKES 16-18 SLICES

Let every day be a sweet celebration

The Pav

The Pav

The Pav took many years to come to fruition.
I owe it to the persistence (and perpetual bloody nagging)
of Courtney and Rachelle.

Courtney's mum is a pavlova queen and so is Rachelle's,
but I just can't handle all the egg whites and refined sugar.

My plant-based version uses chickpea water and raw sugar.
I've figured out the magic method to get it light and fluffy after receiving a long
and extensive voice message one day from Courtney instructing me to:

Leave it in the oven.

Don't touch it when it's in the oven.

You look at it from outside the oven.

Don't open the oven to look at it.

You know what your problem is? You opened the oven. Don't do that.

Cheeky shit that she is.

When I first met Courtney, her father was spending a whole year in the health retreat
where I apprenticed. Courtney was 15 years old at the time. Her father wanted her
to intern at the retreat and spend a week in housekeeping, gardening and the kitchen.

When she arrived in the kitchen I watched her peel carrots for a week while we laughed,
poked fun at each other and became fast friends. Over time we lived together, she became my
PA for a while, and now she tells me how to make my own pavlova after nagging me for years.

Rachelle also begged me to make her a pavlova, so last year I finally gave in.

At our Christmas Eve dinner, I brought it out as a surprise and plonked it
in front of her all decked out on a beautiful crystal cake stand.

She said thank you, then promptly dug her spoon right into the middle of it and started eating.

Classy huh.

I moved on to chat with Jon and Simone at the other end of the table, a moment later,
Rachelle was standing next to me sobbing. I honestly thought something terrible had happened
to her daughter and as I looked up in alarm she said "I'm having a Ratatouille Moment".

I'm like "you're what?"

(If you don't know what a Ratatouille Moment is then
I give you full permission to Google this one).

Rachelle can't eat dairy, but this Pavlova transported her back to every
Christmas she'd had as a child, when her mother would whip up a pavlova for the family.

This is the power and the magic of food. And friends.

Ingredients

FOR PAVLOVA

200ml chickpea water
(a can of 400g chickpeas
contains 200ml of water)
250g raw sugar, powdered
(add your sugar into your
high-speed blender, push
play to turn into powder,
this takes seconds)
100g #COURAGE

FOR SERVING

Fruits of your choice
Coconut yogurt
Maple syrup

PREP TIME 15 mins
BAKING TIME 1h 45 mins
FREEZER-FRIENDLY No
C, RSF, GF, NF, V

Method

Line two standard baking trays (I used pizza trays) with greaseproof paper and set aside.

Whisk the chickpea water with an electric mixer at high speed for 8-10 minutes or until stiff peaks form.

After 8-10 minutes reduce the speed and gradually add the powdered sugar while the mixer is running.

Once you add all the sugar, increase the speed to high again and mix for 5 more minutes or until stiff peaks form.

Turn the oven to the lowest temperature. Mine was 100C / 212F.

Divide the pavlova mixture between the prepared trays. Spread the mixture into a 20-22cm circle and then flatten it until it's around 4cm thick.

Bake for about 1 hour and 45 minutes.

Once done, let the pavlova rest for 10 minutes and cool down.

Decorate with fruits and serve with coconut yogurt and maple syrup.

This is not made out of powdered white sugar and egg whites. So after it's cooked, allow it to cool 10-15 minutes and you have to decorate it immediately as it will deflate (in my experience). If you do leave it before decorating it and it gets sticky and gains moisture, stick it back in the oven on low for about 15 minutes to crisp up and cool before decorating it.

SERVES 6

Doughnuts

Ladies and gentlemen, I present to you doughnuts that are Actually Good For You.
Now go forth and enjoy these to the very last one.

And btw, here's what you do with doughnuts:

Inject some jam into them.

Stick chunks of chocolate into them.

Pipe my Chocolate "Crack" Spread into them.

Or just eat these bad boys exactly the way they are.

Ingredients

FOR THE DOUGH

50g powdered coconut sugar (do this by adding coconut sugar to your highspeed blender and pulsing until the sugar becomes a powder which only takes a few seconds)

300g white spelt flour

15g egg replacement
(I use Bob's Red Mill Egg Replacer)

10g dry instant yeast

180ml plant milk, lukewarm

50ml rice bran oil

15ml apple cider vinegar

A pinch of salt

1L Rice bran oil, for frying

FOR DUSTING

36g powdered coconut sugar

1 tsp cinnamon powder

A pinch of #APPRECIATION

Method

Mix all the dry ingredients until well combined.

In another bowl, whisk the milk, oil, and apple cider vinegar until combined.

Pour into the bowl with the dry mixture and knead until all the ingredients are incorporated. Don't overmix.

Briefly knead the dough and let it rest for 45 minutes in a very warm place.

Once the dough is ready, punch down and divide it into small balls (40 grams each) and let them rise again for 15-20 minutes.

Heat oil in a pan and when it's around 180C/360F hot, place one doughnut in to test the oil is hot enough to cook the doughnut fast and then continue cooking small batches until golden brown. Work in small batches and don't overcrowd the pan.

When the doughnuts are ready, transfer to a plate lined with paper towels.

Mix the coconut sugar and cinnamon powder and dust your fluffy doughnuts.

PREP TIME 20 mins
RESTING TIME 1h
FREEZER-FRIENDLY No
C, RSF, NF, V

MAKES 16 DOUGHNUTS

Dee's Chocolate Mousse

Dee is my incredible assistant here in Bali. She made the executive decision that my chocolate frosting is actually the best chocolate mousse she had ever tasted.

So now you have it.

Welcome to Dee's Chocolate Mousse.

Ingredients

200ml Kara coconut cream
1 tsp vanilla extract
200g 70% dark chocolate, melted
A pinch of salt
Fruits of your choice, for toppings
20ml #PEACE

Method

Add the ingredients to your food processor and process for about 15 seconds or until combined.

Transfer to serving glasses and chill for at least 3 hours.

Top with your favourite fruits and enjoy!

PREP TIME 5 mins
FREEZER-FRIENDLY Yes
R, RSF, GF, NF, V

SERVES 3

Smash one of these open
(there's white gold inside)

Sweet Potato Fudge

Don't be fooled by the sweet potato - just focus on the fudge!
I gotta say it's not my thing, but hey, everyone else loved it so here it is.
This won the People's Choice awards and I listen to my people.

Ingredients

220 grams raw sweet potato, peeled, chopped into chunks and steamed for 10 minutes until little soft to press (cool down completely before using)
120g almond butter
115ml coconut oil, melted
55g cacao powder
50ml maple syrup
40g coconut sugar
1/2 tsp vanilla extract or vanilla paste
A pinch of salt
70g coconut flakes
A pinch of #LOVE

Method

Line a 21.6cm x 11.4cm x 6.35cm tin with unbleached baking paper and set aside.

Add all the ingredients except the coconut flakes to a high-speed blender or food processor.

Blend for about 10 seconds or until the ingredients gets combined and mushy. Do not overmix the batter as the oil will separate.

Add the shredded coconut and stir to incorporate it into the fudge mixture.

Transfer the mixture to the tin, press down firmly and evenly and freeze until it sets.

Cut into little squares and enjoy!

PREP TIME 5 mins
FREEZER-FRIENDLY Yes
C, RSF, GF, V

MAKES 32 SQUARES

Roll it with good intention

Cinnamon Scrolls

Cinnamon Scrolls

Cinnamon Scrolls

Do you remember cinnamon toast?
That's what these Cinnamon Scrolls remind me of.

Life as I knew it stopped after eating one of these,
and even today the smell of baking or even just toast in the toaster
gets me salivating and makes me a little weak at the knees.

Cinnamon Scrolls remind me of times spent walking through my local
shopping centres as a young adult. I would smell cinnamon toast from
the old ladies having a cup of tea and toast after their game of tennis.
There was such a sense of joy and community that surrounded them
and it seemed to float across with the aroma of cinnamon and baking.

These are completely unlike the white sugar shit storm that sits out there
on the shelves of commercial bakeries and supermarkets. Avoid them.
Make these instead. Your body will thank you. Just like your taste buds.

Ingredients

FOR THE DOUGH

350ml plant milk, lukewarm
30g coconut sugar
100ml coconut oil
10g chia seeds, ground
11g dried yeast
600g white spelt flour

FOR THE MIDDLE MIX

80g coconut sugar
150g dried currants
100g walnuts, finely
chopped
2 tsp cinnamon powder
1 tsp salt

FOR BRUSHING

Maple syrup, as much as
needed
10g #PEACE

Method

Line a square or round (I used a round tin 22cm x 4.5cm) baking cake tin with baking paper and set aside.

TO PREPARE THE DOUGH

Add the ingredients to a bowl and mix well.

Knead the dough in a mixer with a dough hook for 8-10 minutes or if you're doing it old school (by hand) you need to knead the dough on a lightly dusted floured clean surface for 8-10 minutes.

Transfer the dough back to the bowl and leave it to rise for 45 minutes to an hour in a warm place.

Dust a clean working surface with flour.

Take the dough out of the bowl and roll it out into a rectangular shape until it's 1/2 cm (0.2 in) thick.

TO PREPARE THE MIDDLE MIX

Combine the ingredients in a bowl and set aside.

Brush the rolled out dough with maple syrup (this will make the mix stick a little).

Sprinkle the middle mix over the dough and press it gently down.

Roll the dough tightly into a log and cut it into 2 inch slices.

Arrange the slices close together in the prepared tin.

Keep the dough in a warm place to allow it to rise again for 45 minutes to an hour.

Preheat your oven to 180C / 356F.

Brush with maple syrup and sprinkle with cinnamon.

Bake in the preheated oven for 25 minutes.

When done, remove and drizzle with lots of maple syrup.

Allow to cool slightly before serving.

PREP TIME 10 minutes
RISING TIME 1.5 hours
BAKING TIME 25 minutes
FREEZER FRIENDLY Yes
C, RSF, V

SERVES 8-12

Everyone is living life, living life with sweets and not feeling guilty doing it. It's about desserts that don't take from your health, they give back, and mostly they bring back those childhood food memories.

Coconut Sugar

Coconut sugar – also known as coconut blossom
sugar – is produced by collecting sweet sap from the
coconut flower. The same palm trees produce coconuts
and are full of breezy, tropical goodness.

In Bali, we call a fresh young coconut
"the never-ending coconut" because the amount
of sweet coconut water never seems to end.

In the same way, when tended carefully,
the flowers continue to produce the sweet sap
which turns into coconut sugar.

Coconut sugar ranks lower on the glycemic index
than many other forms of sugar, which means your
blood sugar levels remain more stable in comparison.

To produce the sugar, the sap is collected by tapping the
coconut blossom and then gently heated to evaporate the
moisture content. It's a gentle process which I love,
because it means the sugar is not highly refined or
processed, and remains very close to its original nature.

As it caramelises, the flavours intensify slightly, lending
a richness and depth to desserts and sweet dishes.

Each mouthful of fresh sap is incredible.
It's truly nature's candy. If only you could
scratch and taste this pic of the fresh sap!

Instead you'll just have to make time to come to
Indonesia and try its mind-blowing flavour yourself.

Throughout this book, I used dried coconut sugar,
which is made through a slightly different process to the
gentle heating and molding of the fresh sap.

Because it's not highly processed and retains
most of its original nutrients, coconut sugar is a rich
brown colour. It also has a delicious, textured aroma as
opposed to the bland sterile smell of refined white sugar.
You can see why I'm a fan.

Black Sticky Rice

Indonesian food culture is warm and welcoming, just like this beautifully sweet and filling Black Sticky Rice. It's one of those sweet, wholesome treats that are not found so easily in cafes. For us at home, it makes the perfect winter sweet dish.

Ingredients

1L water
50g uncooked black sticky rice, soaked for at least 45 minutes and drained
60g uncooked white sticky rice, soaked for at least 45 minutes and drained
100g coconut sugar
A pinch of salt
150ml coconut milk
1-3 drops of Young Living essential orange oil
10ml #FAITH

Method

Add the water, black and white rice to a pot and cook over high heat for 30 minutes. Stir continuously to avoid burning.

Reduce the heat to low and cook for 20 more minutes. Keep stirring continuously.

Stir in the sugar and a pinch of salt and cook for another 10 minutes.

Turn off the heat, put the lid on and leave the pudding to rest for 15-20 minutes (this is the time to add your Young Living essential orange oil).

Warm up the milk with a pinch of salt in another pot and serve with the rice.

SOAKING TIME 45 mins
COOKING TIME 1h
RESTING TIME 15-20 mins
FREEZER-FRIENDLY No
C, RSF, GF, NF, V

SERVES 4

Coconut Cream

When it comes to coconut cream, I'd be lying
if I didn't say fresh is best. But I'd also be
some dreadful food snob if I only used fresh coconut
milk - because I get that not everyone lives on a tropical
island, and even if they do, they might not care.

What is available everywhere is the
Kara brand of coconut milk (also known
as the Ayam brand).

If you can't find Kara or Ayam Cream,
as a general rule find something with the
most "coconut" as possible and the least
amount of stabilisers, oils, fillers,
#fakenews, or sugar added.

Coconut Cream is a rich, decadent cream.
I grew up around coconut trees. I climbed them,
opened coconuts as a kid, I made the milk myself
and I ate out of coconut bowls.

There's a certain kind of magic about coconuts.
The weighty nuts that drop with a crash through the
foliage. The spiky silhouettes of the palm trees in the
fading light of the day. The unpredictable spurt of
coconut water when you pierce the shell.

When you're making the recipes in this book
you can swap out coconut milk for another other
plant-based milk (such as almond or oat milk),
but for coconut cream you're best to stick with Kara
or Ayam Cream brands as they work.

*Invest in your inner health
contract using real ingredients.*

Homemade Jam

Homemade Jam

Nothing is better than Homemade Frikking Jam.
For some reason we got a little sweary over these jars of goodness.

Make it with maple syrup if you like (add a little at a time to get the sweetness
you like). Then cook that bastard down so all the water boils off, and then enjoy
the natural flavours and colours as they become rich and alive.

Put this jam on my Jamdrop cookies. Smear it in between layers of the Big Ass
Chocolate Cake. Have it on toast or jam it up however you want.

Here's the trick btw. You must cook the entire contents down
to a sticky jam texture. Pull up a chair, a book, a glass of wine and some good music
(I use reggae), then prepare to spend some quality time in the kitchen right next to this
jam. The more water you can boil off from this concoction the more flavour you will
liberate (and the longer it will last in the fridge).

Get into it.

Ingredients

FOR THE BLUEBERRY JAM

1kg blueberries, frozen
1 cup coconut sugar
1/4 lime, juiced

FOR THE STRAWBERRY JAM

1kg fresh strawberries, left
whole, green tops removed
1/2 cup coconut sugar
1/4 lime, juiced
100g #COMFORT

Method

Add the berries to two separate pots and pour in the sugar.

Bring to the boil and then cook for 10 minutes on high.

Reduce the heat to low and leave to simmer for 45-60 minutes until the mixture reaches thick, jam-like consistency.

Stir occasionally to prevent the jam from sticking to the bottom of the pots.

Leave the jams to cool completely.

Drizzle with freshly squeezed lime juice and then transfer to glass jars.

The jams keep well in the fridge for up to 2 weeks.

PREP TIME 5 mins
COOKING TIME 1h
FREEZER-FRIENDLY Yes
C, RSF, GF, NF, V

MAKES 400ML

Banana Spring Rolls

*You know those horrible packets of random spring rolls that lurk
in the freezer section of the supermarket?*

You'd never convince me to buy them - let alone make a sweet, healthy version of them!

*But one day my fabulous assistant Dee - the one who keeps me organised, on time and
in fits of laughter all day - announced that "Chef: you should make Banana Spring
Rolls! The ones here in Indo are full of white sugar and bad chocolate. But you could do
it with banana, coconut sugar and cinnamon..."*

*I was like "naaah" - until one day I was walking past the freezer section with the spring
rolls and the thought just wouldn't leave me.*

*So here you have it - Banana Spring Rolls. Only they're not just made with coconut
sugar and cinnamon. I've added a splash of maple syrup and dipped them in coconut
yoghurt for the best damn rolls ever!*

PS - for frying I use rice bran oil, but avocado oil works just as well.

Ingredients

3 bananas, cut into sticks
(like a cigarette stick)
Cinnamon powder, a dash
Coconut sugar, as much as
you like (I used around
1/2 tsp per roll)
1 pack of spring roll
wrapper (containing
10 wrappers)
1L rice bran oil
1 pinch of #LOVE

Method

Place the wrapper in a diamond position.
Place the banana on the bottom and sprinkle
with cinnamon powder and coconut sugar.

Roll up halfway, fold sides in (like a present),
then finish rolling. Repeat until finished.

Fry the rolls in a preheated oil until golden brown.
Transfer onto a paper towel.

Serve with maple syrup and coconut yogurt.

PREP TIME 3-5 mins
COOKING TIME Cook until
golden brown
FREEZER-FRIENDLY No
C, RSF, NF

SERVES 2-3

Roasted Sesame Seed Combo

Peppermint Combo

Next Level Chocolate

My friend Daina made chocolate at home for years using coconut oil, maple and cacao powder. She knows what she's doing, but I have to say when she used this recipe she called me straight away and said "Chef, this is next level. This is Next Level Chocolate".

So here you have it. Next Level Chocolate.

Ingredients

FOR THE BASE

250g cacao butter, finely chopped
200g cacao liquor or paste, finely chopped
150ml maple syrup
1/2 tsp vanilla extract or powder
A pinch of salt
10ml #POSITIVITY

FRUIT AND NUT COMBO

80g roasted walnuts
80g dried currants
100g dried sour cherries

PEPPERMINT COMBO

2 tsp cacao nibs
3 drops of Young Living peppermint oil

ROASTED SESAME SEED COMBO

Black and white sesame seeds, roasted
A pinch of salt

Method

TO PREPARE THE BASE

Add the cacao butter to the top of your double broiler, let it melt and set aside.

Add the cacao paste to the top of the double broiler, melt and set aside.

Tip the melted cacao butter into the cacao paste, add the remaining base ingredients and mix well to incorporate.

Combine the chocolate base with any of the flavour combos.*

Pour into your moulds or spread onto a lined tray and place in the freezer to set.

*I divided the base into three parts. I sprinkled the fruit and nut combo over one, mixed the peppermint combo into the second part, and sprinkled the sesame combo on top of the third part.

PREP TIME 20 mins
FREEZER-FRIENDLY Yes
R, RSF, GF, V

MAKES 550G

Fruit and Nut Combo

Baking is spreading love

Apple Pie

Apple Pie

*I'm so proud to tell you that I totally nailed the crust on this apple pie.
It tastes buttery. And it has NO butter.*

*All my dairy-free mates that love and miss their apple pies are now sorted.
And the world is a better place.*

*And while you're here, I want to share a memory that brought me to tears
as I was simmering the apples and getting them all delicious and caramelly.*

*I remembered my dear dad and the frozen supermarket apple strudels
that he would bring home and heat up. The whole house would smell of
magnificent baked apple and pastry - just like this apple pie.*

Ingredients

FOR THE PIE CRUST

280g white spelt flour

30g coconut sugar

1 tsp salt

110g coconut oil, solid
or frozen and broken
into chunks

120ml ice water

30g #PATIENCE

FOR THE FILLING

1.5kg granny smith apple,
peeled and thinly sliced

1/2 tsp cinnamon powder

1 tsp allspice powder

1/2 vanilla pod, cut into
3 pieces

50ml maple syrup

155g coconut sugar

230ml water

1 tsp cornstarch,
combined with 15ml water

FOR SERVING

Vegan ice cream of
your choice

Method

TO PREPARE THE CRUST

Preheat your oven at 150C / 300F.

Add the flour, sugar, and salt to your food processor and
pulse until combined.

Add the frozen cut up coconut oil and pulse again until the
mixture becomes crumbly.

Pour in the ice water and process again. At this point, the
ingredients will slowly start coming together into a dough.

Transfer the dough to a lightly floured surface and roll it
into a ball.

Divide the dough ball into two pieces and save one for
the top crisscross crust.

Using a rolling pin, roll out one dough ball into a circle
larger than your pie tin.

Transfer the dough to a round 24cm x 3.5cm pie tin lined
with baking paper.

Tuck the crust in along the edges of the tin.

Trim off any excess dough but still keep a little overhang
over the edges of the tin.

Keep the crust in the fridge while you are preparing
the filling.

Method Cont'd

TO PREPARE THE FILLING

Add all the ingredients except the cornstarch to a pot and cook over high heat for 5 minutes.

Make sure the apples are submerged in the liquid and stir constantly to avoid burning. Adjust the heat if needed.

Turn down the heat and cook on medium-low for about 25 minutes until the apples become soft and the liquid turned syrupy.

Turn the heat up and make a hole in the middle by moving the apples to the side of the pot.

Gradually pour in the cornstarch mixture and stir until you get a sticky sauce.

Turn off the heat and allow the filling to rest for 10 minutes.

TO PREPARE THE CRISSCROSS CRUST

Place the saved crust dough on a lightly floured surface and roll it out into a circle larger than your pie tin.

Cut the dough into strips that you will use to make a crisscross pattern on top of the pie.

TO ASSEMBLE THE PIE

Preheat your oven at 150C / 300F.

Pour the filling over the base crust.

Layout the dough strips on top of the filling forming a crisscross pattern.

Roll up and tuck in the overhanging crust and bake in the preheated oven for 45-50 minutes.

Allow to rest and cool down before serving.

PREP TIME 20 mins
BAKING TIME 45-50 mins
FREEZER-FRIENDLY Yes
C, RSF, NF, V

MAKES 8-12 SLICES

Apple Pie

- RAW -
Chocolate Crackles

This is the new version of the old school classic. Chocolate Crackles! Oh the memories.

*Only this time instead of nasty copha, white sugar and rice bubbles,
you've got real food, real flavours, and real nourishment.*

Of course you wouldn't want to eat these every day. Or maybe you would...

Ingredients

200g cacao liquor or paste
250g cacao butter
150ml maple syrup
1/2 tsp vanilla bean paste
A pinch of salt
200g buckwheat, activated (buckinis)
50g shredded coconut
40g desiccated coconut
200g dried currants
A pinch of #COURAGE

Method

Line a large baking tray filled with mini muffin paper cups and set aside.

Melt the cacao paste and cacao butter separately and then mix them together.

Add the maple and a pinch of salt and mix well.

Stir in all the other ingredients and then evenly transfer the mixture to the prepared muffin cups.

Place in the freezer to set and then EAT!

PREP TIME 10 mins
FREEZER-FRIENDLY Yes
R, NF, GF, RSF, V

MAKES 30-35 BITE-SIZE PIECES

White Chocolate Mousse

White Chocolate Mousse

My friend Simone loved this recipe when I first made it.
It's like a cloud of cotton candy in your mouth - sweet, light and full of wonder.
The perfect dessert when you've had a rich dinner but you still want something sweet.

Ingredients

250g white vegan
chocolate, melted*
200ml chickpea water
(a can of 400g chickpeas
contains 200ml of water)
Toppings of your choice
10ml #TRUST

*I used vegan chocolate
sweetened with
coconut sugar.

Method

Strain the chickpeas and keep the water. Use chickpeas for hummus or curry.

Pour the chickpea water into a bowl and mix with an electric mixer for about 8 minutes or until it resembles the white peaks of stiffly beaten egg whites.

When stiff peaks start to form, gradually fold in the melted chocolate till just combined.

Divide the mixture into four small glasses and pop in the fridge to set.

Top with the toppings of your choice and serve.

PREP TIME 10 mins
FREEZER-FRIENDLY Yes
R, RSF, GF, NF, V

SERVES 4

Celebrate your sweet tooth naturally

Maple Syrup

Maple syrup is made from the sap of maple trees.
Period. The end. That's it.

Look out for anything that attempts to pass itself
off as maple syrup. Imposters like "maple-flavoured
syrup", pancake syrup, waffle syrup and other
syrups will attempt to seduce you with their
treacle-coloured caramelly looks but be warned,
they are usually made from processed, high-
fructose corn syrup. Walk away.
Just walk away.

Maple syrup remains very close to nature,
which means our bodies delight in its
flavour and components.

After the sap is collected, it is heated to
remove the moisture while retaining all of the
complex minerals and antioxidants which
yield its distinct flavours.

It's my favourite sweetener to cook with
and I know it feels good in my body.

Life without maple would indeed
be a bitter life.

My Dad's Fruit Cake

Me and my Dad

My Dad's Fruit Cake

*Dad loved fruit cake. He would buy it all year round,
keep it in the fridge and have a slice every now and then with his cuppa.
Makes me smile just writing that sentence.*

*One day dad told me a wonderful story about how his Mum
would make a one-pound fruit cake, wrap in baking paper,
put it in a tight-fitting tin and ask my Dad to weld the sides shut.*

*She would send it off to her other sons and daughters
that were all in the war (Dad was the youngest so he couldn't go).
A little later he became a welder and a panel beater.*

*This story was my Dad's connection to fruit cake.
A food memory that lives inside of him via his Mum's baking.*

*Food is powerful. It has the ability to turn back time and remind us of the
smell and taste of days gone by. It has a magical gift of connecting us instantly
to people, places and things, and in doing so it keeps these memories alive.*

*I know Dad would be proud of this cake, with its boozy flavour and the massive
amount of fruit in it. This recipe reminds me of you, Dad. I miss you so very
much and you will be forever in my heart and mind.*

From your loving daughter, Cyn xx

Ingredients

250g golden raisins,
roughly chopped

250g currants, roughly
chopped

250g sultanas, roughly
chopped

200ml brandy

150ml rice bran oil

250g coconut sugar

30g chia seeds, ground

120g breadcrumbs

125g white spelt flour

A pinch of salt

1 tsp nutmeg

10g allspice

200ml any plant milk

A handful of walnuts,
roughly chopped

100ml #ACCEPTANCE

Method

The night before, add the roughly chopped dried fruits
(I used my food processor on pulse to chop mine) to a bowl,
pour in the brandy, push the fruits down until they are fully
covered. Set aside overnight to soak.

The next day, preheat your oven to 140C / 284F.

Line a round 20.5x6.5cm cake tin with baking paper
and set aside.

Transfer the soaked fruits to a big bowl and add all the other
ingredients except for the walnuts.

Fold gently until the ingredients are well combined.

Transfer to the prepared tin and press down until the mixture
comes together into a solid shape.

Decorate with the chopped walnuts and place a tray filled
with water in the oven while the cake is baking to create
moisture. Bake in the preheated oven for 1 hour and 20
minutes.

When the cake is ready, let it cool down before serving.

SOAKING TIME overnight
PREP TIME 5 mins
BAKING TIME 1h 20 mins
FREEZER-FRIENDLY No
C, RSF, V

SERVES 12-16 SLICES

Peanut Butter

*Two of my mates, John A and Phil, came over on separate occasions and basically
ate a whole jar of peanut butter each while they sat on the couch and talked.*

*They basically spread it on anything that didn't move, and when the crackers and
protein balls and bread ran out they just spooned it naked into their mouths.*

My peanut butter is the best. Want to know how?

In Indonesia, we can get fresh peanuts with the skin on.

*I roast them with the skin on for 10 minutes at a time,
removing them at each interval to give them a good stir.*

*When they are golden brown I let them cool,
then my beautiful friends help me, while gossiping to remove the skin
by gently rubbing them between their hands until the skins fall off.*

*It takes time. And attention. Just watching them do
this very act is the magic ingredients if you ask me.*

I believe in taking my time on moments like this.

(If you can't get peanuts with the skins on you can still take your time).

Ingredients

1kg raw shelled peanuts
(skins off)
1/2 tsp salt
A pinch of #ABUNDANCE

Method

Preheat your oven to 160C / 320F.

Roast the peanuts until lightly golden brown. Check and stir
every 10 minutes to avoid burning (it took me 30 minutes).

Leave to cool and then add to a highspeed blender.

Blend the roasted peanuts and salt for a few minutes until
the peanuts turn into a smooth butter.

Transfer to a jar, leave to cool down completely before
placing the lid on and storing it in the fridge.

PREP TIME 5 mins
COOKING TIME 25-30 mins
FREEZER-FRIENDLY Yes
C, RSF, GF, V

MAKES 1KG

Chocolate Spread

We're calling this Chocolate Spread but we all know this is not a spread, it's Chocolate Crack. Chocolate Crack Spread if you must, but it's basically Crack.

Do not leave this jar unattended. Do not place it where your children play. Do not let your partner know where it is. And if you don't have a partner, be careful who you share this with (unless you want them to become your partner).

I gave a jar to The Great Writer Man to try. He made the mistake of bringing it out at a dinner partner and everyone fell in love - with the Chocolate Crack! Now he has an empty jar and a group of friends that only like him for this Chocolate (Crack) Spread.

I guess in life you win some and you lose some...

You can't lose with this spread though. It's delicious. It's decadent. It's the stuff that dreams are made of.

Ingredients

120ml coconut oil, melted
1/2 tsp vanilla extract
200ml maple syrup
100g raw cacao powder
A pinch of salt
10ml #EASE&FLOW

Method

Add the ingredients to a blender and blend for about 10 seconds. Don't overmix the spread; otherwise, the oil will separate.

Transfer to a glass jar and keep in the fridge for up to 14 days. Or you can use it as a rich pipping situation for any fruit.

PREP TIME 10 sec
FREEZER-FRIENDLY Yes
R, RSF, GF, NF, V

MAKES 250ML

*All my gold and gems are created by my beautiful friend
Christina - she features in my first book.*

Pumpkin Pie

Pumpkin Pie

Growing up between Australia and New Guinea, I had no idea about the legend of pumpkin pie. That task would fall to my American friends years later.

Apparently, pumpkin pie fixes anything. After making this little glory I have to agree.

Ingredients

FOR THE PIE CRUST

140g white spelt flour
12g coconut sugar
1/2 tsp salt
55g coconut oil, solid
or frozen and broken
into pieces
60ml ice water

FOR THE FILLING

700g pumpkin, steamed
and pureed
200ml Kara coconut cream
150ml maple syrup
30g cornflour
10g allspice
1 tsp vanilla extract
1/2 tsp salt
10ml #INSPIRATION

Method

TO PREPARE THE CRUST

Add the flour, sugar, and salt to your food processor and pulse until combined.

Add the frozen coconut oil and pulse again until the mixture becomes crumbly.

Pour in the ice water and process again. At this point, the ingredients will slowly start coming together into a dough.

Transfer the dough to a lightly floured surface and roll it into a ball.

Using a rolling pin, roll out the dough into a circle larger than your pie tin.

Transfer the dough to a round 24x3.5cm pie tin lined with baking paper.

Tuck the crust in along the edges of the tin.

Trim off any excess dough but still keep a little overhang over the edges of the tin.

Keep the crust in the fridge while you are preparing the filling.

TO PREPARE THE FILLING

Preheat your oven at 150C / 300F.

Add the ingredients to your blender and blend until creamy and smooth.

Pour the filling over the crust and gently tap the tin on the table to smoothen out the surface and get rid of the air bubbles.

Bake in the preheated oven for 1 hour.

Leave the pie to rest for about 15 minutes and then keep it in the fridge until it completely cools down.

PREP TIME 15 mins
BAKING TIME 1h
FREEZER-FRIENDLY Yes
C, RSF, NF, V

MAKES 8-12 SLICES

Lamington Fingers

This is the classic Australian road trip snack food. Grab some "lammos" from the bakery for morning tea and we're away - off to the coast or the country for a long weekend.

Lamingtons are also the dessert you grab when you run out of time but still need to qualify as a "good host" in your own home.

These take a little longer to prepare than a trip to the corner store, but they are infinitely better for you.

Ingredients

FOR THE LAMINGTONS

60ml coconut oil
30g chia seeds, ground
1 tsp vanilla extract
200ml plant-based milk of your choice
120g coconut sugar
120g Bob's Red Mill Gluten Free All-Purpose Baking Flour
1 tsp baking powder
A pinch of salt

FOR THE ICING

80g cacao powder
60ml maple syrup
1/2 tsp vanilla extract
80-100ml water
15ml coconut oil
A pinch of salt

FOR COATING

100g desiccated coconut
10g #COURAGE

Method

TO PREPARE THE LAMINGTONS

Preheat your oven to 160C / 320F.

Combine the coconut oil, chia, vanilla, milk, and sugar and set aside.

In a separate bowl, mix together the flour and baking powder.

Gradually pour the wet mixture into the dry one and stir briefly until combined. Don't overmix the batter.

Transfer to a square 27.5x18x3cm rectangle tray lined with baking paper.

Spread the batter evenly and bake in the preheated oven for 8-12 minutes.

Check the cake and if it's still not slightly golden and springy to touch, bake it for 5-8 more minutes.

Leave the cake to cool completely in the tin and then slice it into pieces of the desired size.

TO PREPARE THE ICING

Whisk together all the ingredients until well combined.

Dip each cake slice into the icing to coat all the sides.

Toss with the coconut and serve.

PREP TIME 10 mins
BAKING TIME 18-20 mins
FREEZER-FRIENDLY Yes
C, RSF, GF, NF, V

MAKES 20 SMALL LAMINGTONS

Carrot Cake

Carrot Cake

They said: It's about the icing Chef, not the cake.

I said: Yeah but the cake needs to be packed with isms and goodness and not be light and fluffy.

They said: who cares about the cake, it's the icing that makes it great.

What can I say? This cake is all about the icing. (And the cake).

Ingredients

FOR THE CAKE MIX

30g chia seeds, ground
60ml maple syrup
145g dried dates
200ml water
150ml coconut oil, melted
350ml plant-based milk
1 tsp vanilla extract
250g grated carrots
1 tsp cinnamon powder
1 tsp nutmeg, freshly grated
or powdered
2 tsp allspice powder
200g Bob's Red Mill Gluten-
Free All-Purpose
Baking Flour
2 tsp baking powder
50g desiccated coconut
100g walnuts, whole
120g raisins
50g coconut sugar
A pinch of salt

FOR THE ICING

150g cashew nuts,
soaked for at least 2 hours
200g white chocolate
(plant-based white
sugar-free), melted
45ml freshly squeezed
lemon juice
300ml Kara coconut cream
10g nutritional yeast, optional
A pinch of salt
100ml #POSITIVITY

PREP TIME 15 mins
BAKING TIME 40-55 mins
FREEZER-FRIENDLY Yes
C, RSF, GF, V

Method

TO PREPARE THE CAKE MIX

Preheat your oven to 170C / 340F.

Add the first seven ingredients to your food processor
and pulse until well combined.

Transfer to a bowl, add the grated carrot, mix well
and set aside.

In a separate bowl, combine the spices, flour,
baking flour, coconut, walnuts, raisins, sugar, and salt.

Fold the wet mixture into the dry one and transfer the
batter to a round 20.5cm x 6cm springform tin lined
with baking paper.

Bake in the preheated oven for 40-55 minutes,
depending on your oven.

Once done, allow to cool completely.

TO PREPARE THE ICING

Add the ingredients except the melted chocolate
to your blender.

Blend until completely smooth and creamy.

Gradually pour in the melted chocolate and blend
for 5 more seconds.

Transfer to a bowl and keep in the fridge for 30 minutes
for the icing to firm up a little ready for icing the cake.

Once the cake is ready and cooled down, flood it with
icing, decorate and serve.

MAKES 18-20 SLICES

The difference between weeds
and flowers is judgement

Mum's Quick Treat for the Kids

Let me introduce you to Kymba, my amazing designer who has an incredible brand called Soulful Branding and is the graphic designer who put together this book and my last one: Plant-Based Love Stories.

She is one of the humans that can take my isms (design) and make it GREAT. She is a soulful genius.

One day over the phone we were going through her amazing designs and I could hear her kids in the background. As we were talking about the recipes she took a deep breath and said "You know what would be cool Chef? How about you create something that I really need - a quick dessert for busy mums like me that you can throw together with stuff in the pantry. Something to keep the kids happy that doesn't take all afternoon to put together".

I thought nothing of it for weeks until one day I had friends coming round and I was in that same position as Kymba... so I threw together this brilliant quick treat that I dedicate to my dear friend and colleague who has two sweet kids that love a little celebration at home every now and then.
Love ya Kymba xxx

Ingredients

20g raw oats
Hot water
A pinch of salt
1 tbsp desiccated coconut
Chocolate chips,
as much as you like
1 tbsp peanut butter
A splash of maple syrup
10g of #PEACE

Method

In a small jar, add in oats, and a pinch of salt. Add the hot water just until the oats are covered.

Top with desiccated coconut, chocolate chips, peanut butter and a splash of maple syrup.

Serve as your quick treat when your stuck for something to make.

PREP TIME 3-5 mins
FREEZER-FRIENDLY No
R, RSF

SERVES 1

Cacao

*If you are new to the idea of cacao paste, welcome to all its glory.
What is it? It's the natural product of ground cacao nibs,
which comes from the fruit of the Theobroma cacao tree.
Cacao paste (also called cacao liquor) is made by roasting the nibs
lightly and crushing them into a liquid. This liquid quickly solidifies at
room temperature and the result is glorious cacao paste. BOOM!*

*Now, what can I say about this cacao drink? It's so good, it can also be
found in my first book Plant-based Love Stories.*

*It warms your soul with its chocolate fragrance holding hands with the
sweetness of maple and the decadent creaminess of coconut milk.*

*Wrap yourself in a blanket and treat your soul with a mug of this
amazing drink.*

Ingredients

45g cacao paste,
chopped roughly
450ml coconut milk
Maple syrup, as much as
you like
A pinch of salt
1 tbsp #ACCEPTANCE

Method

Add everything to a blender and blend until well combined.

Transfer to a small pot, cook on low and keep stirring
continuously to make sure it doesn't burn.

Serve hot.

PREP TIME 2 mins
COOKING TIME 8-10 mins
FREEZER-FRIENDLY No
C, RSF, NF

SERVES 2

Patience is hard, but its fruit is sweet.

My Mum's Fruit Salad

My Mum's Fruit Salad

My mum made the best fruit salad ever. It took me years to appreciate,
and like every ungrateful daughter I thought it just tasted "blah" at the time.

Now that I'm grown up I can fully celebrate her version of a fruit salad.

I called mum to ask why she did it the way she does.
We had a great chat about many things (including fruit salad). I miss her.

She sent me an email later and this was the gist:

Fruit salads seem to have gone out of fashion these days. Probably because they get diluted
with lots of mildly flavoured fruits such as watermelon, honeydew, or rockmelon.

My essential ingredients for an old-fashioned tropical fruit salad are lots of purple
passionfruit (not the "Panama" variety) and a small, golden,
Australian smooth-leaf pineapple (not the big green looking variety from Hawaii).

The blend of these two flavours is the perfect base for a Tropical Fruit Salad.
Add other fruits like red apples and navel oranges, a small amount of banana
(goes brown), red grapes, seeded cherries, nectarines and peaches, etc.
(whatever is in season). Make each piece of fruit a large bite-size piece.

The way you prepare the pineapple is very important. People are lazy and just cut the skin so
thickly that you cut out all the prickles. This is very wasteful. It is much better to cut a normal
thickness of skin and then hold the pineapple on the end of a fork and cut out each row of prickles
with a deep V cut, making sure to get all the prickle out or they will give you a very sore tongue.

Then pulp half the pineapple with a fork down to the core, then cut the rest of the pineapple into
slices and wedges, being careful not to include any of the core, which also gives you a sore tongue.

Leave the Fruit Salad in the fridge for a couple of hours to blend all the flavours.

Small disclaimer: I didn't make it her way (kids these days eh?) cos I had all this random
fruit from shooting all the incredible real food desserts in this book.

I basically used the fruit that I had, which I know mum would appreciate
as she hates wasting food.

We'll leave the last word to Mum:

Hi Cyn, I have just been to see Aunty Ione, and then watched a film with Pat.
It was called "Walkabout". A famous Aussie film, made back in the 1970s.

Yes, I was famous for my tropical fruit salad. Then one day, when I couldn't find a fresh,
small, sweet, smooth-leaf pineapple from the market, I made it with canned pineapple.
One lady told everybody, and then nobody ate it, so that was my final swan song!

You know what to do :)

Enjoy!

Ingredients

1 banana, sliced
1/2 pineapple, chopped
into bite-size chunks
2 passion fruit
A handful of
blackberries
A handful of fresh figs,
cut into quarters
A handful of
strawberries,
cut into quarters
A handful of raspberries
A squish of lime
10g #LOVE

Method

Add all ingredients to a bowl and toss to combine.

Serve immediately and enjoy!

PREP TIME 10 mins
FREEZER-FRIENDLY No
R, RSF, GF, NF,

SERVES 2-4

Cherry and the Ripe

*On rare occasions, my Mum and Dad would buy a single Cherry Ripe bar.
They would proceed to cut it into 4 pieces and share them amongst themselves, my brother
and me while I would sit there quietly trying to figure out which piece was the biggest.*

*For the life of me I wondered why Mum only brought one Cherry Ripe bar
and cut it into 4 instead of buying 4 bars for 4 people?*

*While I was writing this book I called her up and asked her.
In her infinite wisdom she said "Cynthia, it's all we needed.
We didn't need more than a little piece every now and then."*

*In a world where more is more, it's wonderful to be reminded
that less is actually more.*

Ingredients

FOR THE BASE

75g coconut flakes
45g pumpkin seeds
40g sunflower seeds
40g black sesame seeds
40g white sesame seeds
30g chia seeds
140g dried sour cherries
1 tsp vanilla extract
30ml coconut oil, melted
60ml maple syrup
30g oats
15ml water
A pinch of salt
20g grated beetroot

FOR THE TOPPING

350g vegan chocolate,
melted
100g #INSPIRATION

Method

Add all the base ingredients to your food processor.

Process for 30 seconds until well combined and sticky. Scraping down the sides if needed.

Transfer the mixture to a square 27.5x18x3cm rectangle tray lined with baking paper.

Press down firmly to distribute the mixture evenly.

Slice into bars and then keep in the freezer to set.

Dip the bars into the melted chocolate and arrange them on a wire rack to set.

PREP TIME 5 mins
FREEZER-FRIENDLY Yes
R, RSF, NF, V

MAKES 15-20 BARS

Sweets help you fall in love
with the life you already have

Magnum Icecreams

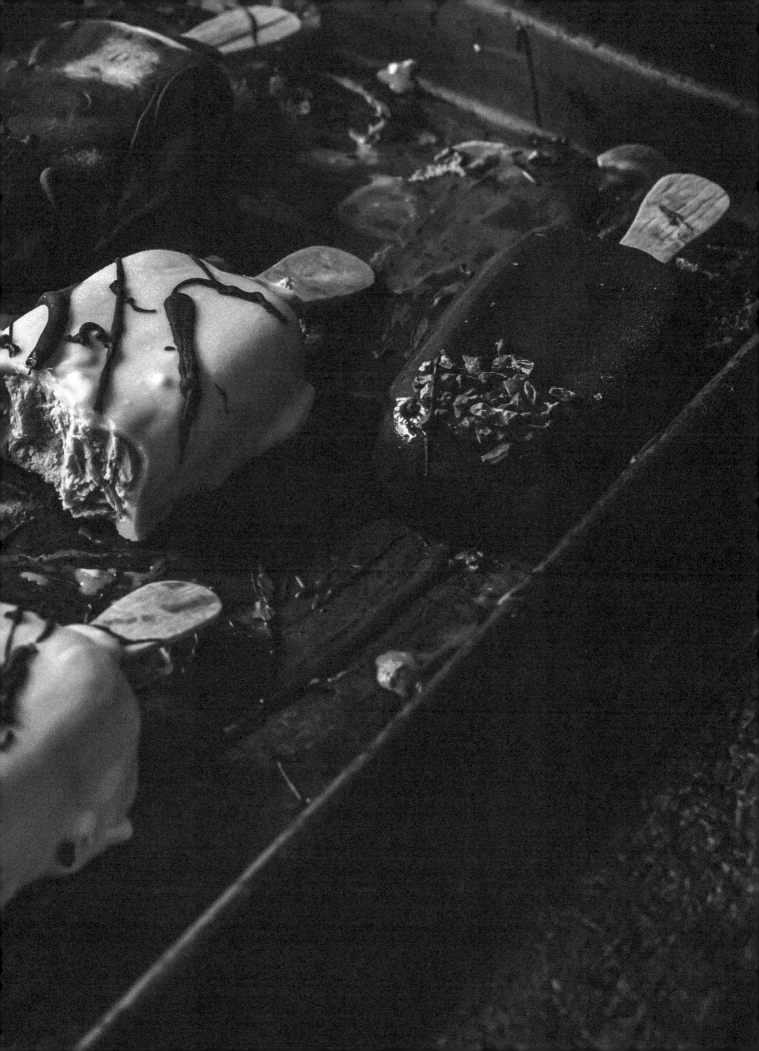

Magnum Icecreams

I have a confession. I made these icecreams for all my vegan friends (that are actually vegan).

Guys - knock yourselves out. It's not my scene but I love you and your wonderful ways.

Judging by your wide eyes, your yums of appreciation and the way you fought over the last icecream I'm pretty happy you'll never look anywhere else for an icecream again.

Welcome to my plant-based Magnums.

Ingredients

FOR THE STRAWBERRY MAGNUM

150g strawberry jam
1 thin slice fresh beetroot
200ml Kara coconut cream
A pinch of salt

FOR THE CHOCOLATE MAGNUM

300ml Kara coconut cream
70ml maple syrup
15g cacao powder

FOR THE CHOCOLATE PEPPERMINT CRUNCH

300ml Kara coconut cream
15g cacao powder
70ml maple syrup
2 drops of peppermint oil
10g cacao nibs

FOR COATING

200g 80% vegan dark chocolate*
30ml #EASE&FLOW

*This is enough to coat 4-5 ice creams.

Method

TO PREPARE THE BASE

Add the ingredients to a highspeed blender and blend on high until well combined.

Pour the mixture into your magnum moulds and freeze overnight.

Remove the ice creams from the moulds and arrange them on a tray lined with baking paper.

Return the ice creams to the freezer while you are preparing the coating.

TO PREPARE THE COATING

Melt the chocolate over low heat.

Allow to cool down a bit before you start coating the ice creams.

Gently dip the ice creams into the melted chocolate and then return them to the freezer for about 30 minutes before serving.

PREP TIME 5 mins
FREEZER-FRIENDLY Yes
R, RSF, GF, NF, V

MAKES 3-4 EACH FLAVOUR
DEPENDING ON THE SIZE OF YOUR MOULDS

Very Vegan Berry Cheesecake

This is the classic Vegan Cheesecake situation.
A chewy crust, a cream-"cheesey" filling, and all the plant-based goodness
you can possibly handle. It's the original vegan, plant-based situation
that's been around for years.

Ingredients

FOR THE BASE

40g oats
30g shredded coconut
100g dried dates
60g sunflower seeds
60g sesame seeds
30ml water
A pinch of salt

FOR THE FILLING

250g cashew nuts, soaked
for at least 2 hours
10g nutritional yeast
1 lemon, juiced
120ml maple syrup
120ml water
A pinch of salt
130g cacao butter, melted
20ml #ACCEPTANCE

FOR TOPPINGS

Any of my homemade
berry jams

Method

TO PREPARE THE BASE

Line a round 24cm x 3.5cm springform cake tin with baking paper and set aside.

Add the ingredients to a food processor and process until sticky and completely combined.

Transfer to the prepared cake tin, press the mixture to distribute it evenly, press down firmly to form a flat base and set aside.

TO PREPARE THE FILLING

Add the ingredients except the melted cacao butter to your blender and blend until creamy and completely smooth.

Add the cacao butter and blend for 20 more seconds.

Pour the filling over the cake base and top with any of my homemade jams.

Place the cake in the fridge and allow to set for 1-2 hours before serving.

PREP TIME 12-15 mins
FREEZER FRIENDLY Yes
R, RSF, GF, V

MAKES 12-16 SLICES

Banana Bread

I was doing a retreat on water fasting and the team helping me insisted on banana bread.

*It was my friend Rana who introduced me to the use of flax seeds in baking.
She was vegan (at the time) and showed me how flax seeds can replace eggs in a recipe.*

So now you have it – my plant-based banana bread.

Ingredients

30g whole flax seeds
150ml water
350g ripe bananas, mashed
220g Bob's Red Mill
Gluten Free All-Purpose
Baking Flour
150ml coconut oil, melted
100ml plant-based milk
10ml vanilla extract
180g coconut sugar
1 tsp baking soda
1 1/2 tsp baking powder
A dash of cinnamon powder
A pinch of salt
100g #SELFWORTH

Method

Combine the flax seeds with water in a small bowl and let it sit for 5-8 minutes.

Preheat your oven to 170C / 340F.

Add all the remaining ingredients to a large bowl and mix until well combined.

Stir in the flaxseed mixture.

Transfer the batter to an 8 cavity rectangle mini bread loaf tin lined with greaseproof paper.

Bake in the preheated oven for 55 minutes.

When done, allow the bread to rest for 10 minutes in the tin and then transfer it to a wire rack to cool completely.

PREP TIME 10 mins
BAKING TIME 55 mins
FREEZER-FRIENDLY Yes
C, RSF, GF, NF, V

MAKES 15-20 SLICES

The best Mantra Thank You Thank YOU

Jayman's Cake

Jayman's Cake

Back when my son Jayman was a teenager he had a problem. He STANK!

For all the Mums and Dads of teenage boys out there, I'm sure you've had the experience of opening your darling boy's bedroom door and being blown back by a haze of hormones and teen spirit.

So why was Jayman so stinky? Because he had a Sugar Addiction. He was non-stop on the sugary lollies while I was being a real food chef.

But you know what? Challenge accepted. I set about finding a way to satisfy his sweet tooth. I didn't want to deprive him. I wanted to nourish him. And to do that I had to meet him where he was and celebrate his sweet tooth naturally.

I began with a wholefood version of his favourite cake - a raspberry chocolate ganache he used to get from the local bakery.

It wasn't easy I can tell you - but apparently, teenage boys are not meant to be easy.

I don't know how many versions I made trying to get it to his standards. He's got good taste, my son, and like a lot of kids, there is no pulling the wool over his eyes. The chocolate ganache was often pushed aside with a "All I can taste is avocado Mum. Yuk!"

Each word was a dagger in my heart, but I knew he was telling the truth.

So many kids want something sweet but they are sensitive to our modern diet of refined and processed food. My niece is gluten- and dairy-intolerant and my heart went out to her too. These kids want to eat fun food, and I was determined to make this a reality for them.

I wanted to show them that being healthy is about having a connection with nature. I didn't want to push them in the wellness industry world of fad diets, or something so restrictive that they would rebel against it later.

So I persevered.

I took my tried and trusted recipes and pushed them and pushed them. Like many works of art this was a real process and it took many exchanges of cruel words and tears before I got it right.

But this pressure to produce the 'impossible' ended up making magic possible! Despite the challenges so much joy and love came from the process. It brought my Jayman and I closer together. And situations of glory were born.

So after much blood, sweat and tears, I am deeply proud to present the Chocolate Raspberry Ganache cake as Jayman's cake.

I feature this cake in my online Cooking Class Series: Celebrate Your Sweet Tooth (Naturally) and I'm grateful to Jayman for the inspiration that he's been.

Ingredients

FOR THE CAKE

200g sunflower seeds,
activated
150g dried dates
40g cacao powder
70g desiccated coconut
30ml water

FOR THE GANACHE

1-2 avocados (I used one
big avocado)
140g dried dates
80g cacao powder
60ml maple syrup
A pinch of salt

FOR THE TOPPINGS

350g frozen raspberries
200g vegan 80% dark
chocolate, melted
100g #CONTENTMENT

PREP TIME 20 mins
FREEZER-FRIENDLY Yes
R, GF, NF, RSF, V

Method

TO PREPARE THE CAKE

Line a round 22cm cake tin with baking paper and set aside.

Add all ingredients to a food processor and process until well combined and sticky resembling a dough type texture.

Transfer the mixture to the prepared cake tin, press evenly and set aside in the fridge to chill.

TO PREPARE THE GANACHE

Add all ingredients to a food processor and process until completely smooth and creamy.

Taste and add more sweetener if needed.

Spread the mixture roughly over your cake.

Top with the frozen raspberries and then drizzle with the melted chocolate.

Transfer to the fridge to firm up a bit.

MAKES 8-12 SLICES

Peanut Butter Slice

*I used to make this recipe with almond butter until I moved to Bali
and found myself on an island literally covered in peanuts.*

*Almonds are imported here. Plus they cost like $500,000 per kilo and I know
they've been sitting in a warehouse for weeks before they get to my table.*

*While I was fixated on almonds, I would hear a little bell outside my house every day.
There walked a man who was at least 80 years old, balancing a pole with buckets of
peanuts at each end and ringing a small bicycle bell.*

*One day I talked to him and discovered he grew them on his farm to sell in the streets of
Sanur. I bought a kilo of his fresh, locally grown peanuts, roasted them, and immediately
changed my old recipe to this one.*

*Wherever possible I use what is local and fresh. If you happen to be living on an
island covered in almonds, or hazelnuts, or even macadamia nuts then half your luck.
Feel free to make this recipe your own as well.*

Ingredients

FOR THE BASE

220g raw pecans, activated
80g desiccated coconut
1/4 tsp cinnamon powder
1 tsp vanilla extract
15g psyllium husk
100g dried dates
30ml water
A pinch of salt

FOR THE FILLING

200ml coconut oil, melted
140g peanut butter, smooth
60ml maple syrup
2 tsp vanilla extract
A pinch of salt

FOR THE TOPPING

300g vegan 70% dark
chocolate, melted
A pinch of salt
A handful of roasted
skinned peanuts
20ml #FORGIVENESS

PREP TIME 10-15 mins
FREEZER FRIENDLY Yes
R, GF, RSF, V

Method

TO PREPARE THE BASE

Add all the ingredients to your food processor and
process until combined and sticky.

Transfer the mixture to a square 27.5x18x3cm rectangle
tray lined with baking paper.

Press the mixture to distribute it evenly, press down
firmly to form a flat base. and set aside.

TO PREPARE THE PEANUT BUTTER FILLING

Add the ingredients to your high-speed blender
and blend on high for 20 seconds until combined.

Pour the mixture over the peanut butter base.
Put in the freezer to set.

When set, flood with the melted chocolate and
roasted peanuts and keep in the fridge until the
chocolate sets.

Cut into squares and serve.

MAKES 30 SMALL SQUARES

Passionfruit Cheesecake

Every time I make a fruity anything
reminds me of my dear friend Valerie

Passionfruit Cheesecake

This is a crowd-pleaser for the non-chocolate lover.
Tangy, tart and sweet as a passionfruit should be.

Ingredients

FOR THE FILLING

8 fresh passionfruit*
250ml maple syrup
230g cashew nuts, soaked for 8 hours
50ml lime juice
200g cacao butter, melted

*Use 1 passionfruit with the seeds and for the remaining 7 passionfruit, strain and discard the seeds. You will need around 200ml of passionfruit juice.

FOR THE BASE

75g sunflower seeds
25g white tahini
65g desiccated coconut
15ml water
1 Tbs psyllium husk
100g dried dates
50g #GRATITUDE

Method

TO PREPARE THE FILLING

Add the ingredients except for the melted cacao butter to a highspeed blender and blend on high until smooth.

Pour in the melted butter and blend for 10 more seconds.

Let the filling rest while you prepare the base.

TO PREPARE THE BASE

Add the ingredients to your food processor and process until well combined and sticky.

Transfer to a loose-bottom 34.5cm x 11cm x 2.5cm rectangular tart tin lined with baking paper.

Press the mixture to distribute it evenly, press down hard to form a flat base.

Top the base with the filling and store into the fridge till it is well firmed up.

PREP TIME 10 mins
FREEZER-FRIENDLY Yes
R, RSF, GF, V

MAKES 8-10 SLICES

Chocolate

Chocolate is life. It's everything.

Throw me a chocolate and no one gets hurt.

Especially if I'm on my period.

Don't come near me unless you have chocolate if that's the case.

And btw – we're not going to talk about that supermarket shit. There's only good chocolate and great chocolate.

The difference between good and great is the organic or biodynamic soil it's grown in. The way it's fermented. The care in which it's roasted.

All chocolate is based on a blend of fat, sweetener and cacao. Commercial chocolate uses dairy as fat and refined white sugar as the sweetener.

The chocolate I choose is much more exquisite. It's plant-based, which means coconut milk instead of cow milk. Palm or coconut sugar instead of refined white sugar. And it's locally grown, harvested and processed.

So choose your chocolate with care. Not only are you ensuring a great recipe, you're supporting farmers, good farming practises, local economies, and real people.

As you embark on the culinary journey that begins with 40% chocolate and ends around 95%, you're essentially reducing the amount of fat and sweetener, and increasing the cacao fat.

How it feels in your body is what you become attuned to.

80% chocolate can be too bitter, or it can be life affirming (especially in my Next Level Chocolate).

45% is creamy and sweet.

At 55% and above, the different notes in the cacao start to come through. Dark, smoky, or with hints of cinnamon, vanilla, currants or berries, every bean is different – just like you.

Chocolate is a journey, but it's also an invitation – to become present right here in the #now.

A little note about white chocolate.

Whispers: It's not really chocolate.

There's less than 20% cacao in most white chocolate. The one I have used throughout this book has 29% cacao butter which has a very mild taste, and the rest of white chocolate is a delicious blend of natural fats and sweeteners.

White chocolate has its place – especially in something like my White Chocolate & Hazelnut Cookies.

But it's not really chocolate (I said it again).

So here we are talking about chocolate when we could be eating it.

You know what to do...

Rustic Chocolate Bar

I have 3 favourite recipes in this book. You've found one of them right here.

*Rich, epic, and chocolatey, I originally popped them in the dehydrator
and meant to set a timer for 6 hours but I left them there overnight!*

*When I pulled them out the next day they were hard as a rock
and I thought they were gone.*

*I left them on the counter to do other things and then,
walking past I snapped off a piece to try.*

*They were Really good. So I covered them in chocolate crack spread
and stuck them in the fridge. Within a week they were gone.*

Ingredients

80g almond meal
20g chia seeds, ground
85g desiccated coconut
75g cacao powder
1/2 tsp baking soda
150ml maple syrup
1 tsp apple cider vinegar
1 tsp vanilla extract
A pinch of salt
30ml #TRUST

Method

Mix together the dry ingredients and set aside.

In a separate bowl, whisk together the wet ingredients.

Fold the two mixtures together, transfer onto a dehydrator sheet* and then spread evenly until the layer is about 1cm thick.

Dehydrate at 42C / 107F for 4 hours than remove carefully from the sheet and flip onto the wire mash rack and dehydrate for an additional 3-4 hours.

Leave the bars to cool down and then serve them with my chocolate crack spread or melted chocolate.

*I used my 9-tray Excalibur dehydrator but any dehydrator you have will work.

PREP TIME 5 mins
DEHYDRATING TIME 6-8h
FREEZER-FRIENDLY No
C, RSF, GF, V

MAKES 12-18 SQUARES

Mango Coconut Muffins

The first time I made these for the test kitchen, our photographer GG finished the plate before we had a chance to properly try them.

Mango Coconut Muffins. What's not to like?

Ingredients

350g fresh ripe mango, roughly cut into 3cm squares
200ml coconut oil, melted
300ml coconut milk or any plant-based milk of your choice
100g coconut butter
50g coconut flakes
130g coconut sugar
20g chia seeds, ground
200g white spelt flour
100ml maple syrup
1 1/2 tsp baking powder
1 tsp vanilla extract
A pinch of salt
30g #RESPECT

Method

Preheat your oven to 170C / 340F.

Add all the ingredients to a large bowl and mix until well combined. Don't overmix the batter.

Pour the batter into a 12-muffin tin lined with greaseproof paper.

Bake in the preheated oven for 25-35 minutes.

When done, allow to cool in the tin before serving.

PREP TIME 8-10 mins
BAKING TIME 25-35 mins
FREEZER-FRIENDLY No
C, RSF, NF, V

MAKES 12 LARGE MUFFINS

Candy Nuts

Candy Nuts

Who doesn't like candied nuts?

They are a favourite at pubs and bars all around the world and the most delicious combination of sweetness and crunch which adds to the roasted nutty flavour.

This moorish treat is perfect for a quick snack on the go or for resting by your hands with a good book on a quiet evening.

Make a large batch and keep them in a glass jar in the fridge for those times you need a quick treat to keep you going.

As always, choose some high quality vanilla essence and some high quality salt - it will make a huge difference to the flavour.

Just be careful you save some for later or they'll all be gone.

Ingredients

200g walnut, roasted no salt
100g cashew, roasted no salt
100g coconut sugar
100ml water
1 tsp vanilla extract

Method

Preheat your oven to 150C / 302F and roast the nuts for 10-15 minutes.

In a pot, add in your sugar, water, vanilla, and salt over high heat, bring to the boil while constantly stirring. Turn the heat to low simmer.

Cook for about 8 minutes until it turns into a thick syrup consistency.

Add in the nuts and cook for another minute. Mix well until all is coated with the caramel.

Transfer to a baking paper and sprinkle with salt. Let cool completely before you put them anywhere near your mouth.

Store in a glass jar in the fridge.

ROASTING TIME 10 mins
COOKING TIME 8-10 mins
FREEZER-FRIENDLY No
C, RSF, GF, V

MAKES 300G

How the French eat cake, like its a romance with a lover...
eaten slowly with an open heart and a delicious smile

The Big Ass Chocolate Cake

The Big Ass Chocolate Cake

*When I revealed this magnificent situation of glory
to the world, everyone was in awe.*

I mean – it's so big.

People were a bit intimidated at first.

"How do we cut it?"

"How many layers is it?"

"Is it all chocolate?"

*You'll also need to stand guard with a wooden spoon to
stop people from plucking berries from the top.*

But I tell you what - for every special occasion, this is the one they want.

*It makes a statement that says "We're here to CELEBRATE".
There's no place for anything but having fun, loving your friends
and celebrating life with this cake.*

*Get into it. The Big Ass Chocolate Cake. Because life is
meant to be enjoyed, every way you can.*

*PS If you have any leftover Big Ass Chocolate Cake make them into cake
balls. Yep cake balls! My mate Kittea placed leftover cake into a bowl and
with her hands re-mushed up the cake and then rolled them into balls...
AKA cake balls. #genius*

Ingredients

FOR THE CAKE

300ml rice bran oil
230g beetroot, finely grated
900ml plant milk
2 tsp vanilla extract
550g coconut sugar
600g Bob's Red Mill
Gluten Free All-Purpose
Baking Flour, sifted
150g cacao powder, sifted
30g chia seeds, ground
30g baking powder, sifted

FOR THE FROSTING

700ml Kara thick
coconut cream
400g 80% dark chocolate,
melted (or any chocolate
of your choice)
100g #PATIENCE

1 batch of my
Homemade Jam

Method

TO PREPARE THE CAKE

You will need four cake tins.

Preheat your oven to 170C / 340F.

Line four, round 22cm x 4cm cake tins with baking paper and set aside.

Add the oil, beetroot, milk and vanilla to a blender and blend to combine.

In a bowl, mix together the dry ingredients.

Gradually add the wet mixture to the dry one and mix until combined and there are no lumps. Don't overmix the batter.

Pour the batter into the prepared tins and bake them for 25 minutes.

Once done, allow the cake to cool down before removing it from the tin. Then transfer onto a wire rack to cool completely.

TO PREPARE THE FROSTING

Add the coconut cream to your food processor and press Play.

While the processor is running, gradually drizzle in the melted chocolate and process for 10 seconds.

Transfer to a bowl and let the frosting sit in the fridge allow it to firm up a little so its easy to spread and is ready to be used.*

Generously cover the layers of the cake with frosting and my Homemade Jam.

*The frosting will keep for 5 days in the fridge if you don't use it all.

PREP TIME 5 mins
BAKING TIME 25 mins
C, GF, RSF, NF, V

SERVES 10-12

Blackcurrant and Strawberry Crumble Slice

This crumble slice is in honour of my good mate Kate, who grew up in country Victoria playing tennis as a young girl.

Every Saturday the "tennis club ladies" would put on a spread of sandwiches, drinks and sweets for lunch and afternoon tea.

The jam crumble was Kate's favourite and it just made her wild with excitement. She reckons the recipe was probably from one of those old Women's Weekly magazines.

My version tastes just as good, with the timeless combination of flavours, home-made jam and a biscuity base.

Here's to childhood memories of growing up in the country. Here's to Kate for nagging me to make this beauty. Love ya Kate.

Ingredients

FOR THE JAM

300g frozen strawberry
300g frozen blackcurrant
175ml maple syrup
1 tsp vanilla extract
2 tsp cornflour
15ml water

CRUST AND CRUMBLE

300g almond meal
15g cornflour
100ml coconut oil
80ml maple syrup
1 tsp vanilla extract
A pinch of salt
1ml of #FORGIVENESS

Method

FOR THE JAM

In a small pot, add in the frozen berries, maple syrup, and cook on a gentle simmer for around 20 minutes while constantly stirring.

In a small bowl, mix the cornflour and water. to make a slurry. Add to the simmering berries along with the vanilla, and stir. Cook for another minute.

Turn the heat off and let cool.

FOR THE CRUST AND CRUMBLE

Preheat your oven to 160C.

In a bowl, mix all of the ingredients until well combined.

Separate 250g of the mixture and set aside.

Transfer remaining mixture to a 23cm x 22cm x 5cm rectangle tray lined with baking paper. Press gently to make a base.

Bake for 10 minutes.

Remove from the oven and add the jam evenly on top. Sprinkle the reserved crumble mixture, and bake for another 20 minutes.

Let rest and serve.

PREP TIME 8-10 mins
BAKING TIME 30 mins
FREEZER-FRIENDLY Yes
C, GF, RSF

MAKES 8-12 SLICES

Oats

Working in health retreats many years ago,
I was taught a great way to use oats. I would grab
handfuls of oat groats and cast them into the soil.
As they grew they would bind nitrogen to the soil,
replenishing it for future crops. How genius is that.
Not just for cake bases and porridge eh?

I sometimes wonder what it was like 200 years,
maybe even 2000 years ago. Because oats are an
ancient grain. Whole civilisations have been kept
alive on oats. Armies and citizens and whole cities
would have slow-cooked porridge for breakfast,
grown from rich and fertile soils.

Nowadays we think instant oats take too long!

But good things take time.

Time to prepare, time to eat, and time
for the soil to replenish.

That's why I like oats - they nourish our bodies
and they nourish the soil.

I use them in porridge, granola bars,
as the bases for raw cakes, to make milk,
and so much more.

Oats are like a little hug on the inside.
They make you feel secure. Nourished. Content.
They are a wonderful way to start the day, and a
wonderful way to end the day.

Happy Mother's Day cake

Strawberry Coconut Cream Pie

Strawberry Coconut Cream Pie

Tangy, Strawberry-ey, sweet, creamy, and feminine.

This is the perfect sweet for your women's / sisterhood / Goddess circle, an elegant afternoon tea, or when you want to impress the ladies in your life.

Ingredients

FOR THE BASE

150g sunflower seeds
50g white tahini
130g desiccated coconut
30ml water
10g psyllium husk
200g dried dates

FOR THE FILLING

200ml Kara coconut cream
600g fresh strawberries
10g fresh beetroot
150ml maple syrup
200g cashew nuts, soaked for 8 hours
250g cacao butter, melted
A pinch of #ACCEPTANCE

FOR THE TOPPING

As much of my strawberry jam as you like

Method

TO PREPARE THE BASE

Add the ingredients to your food processor and process until combined and sticky.

Transfer to a round spring form tin lined with baking paper.

Press to distribute evenly and form a flat base.

TO PREPARE THE FILLING

Add everything except cacao butter to a blender and blend until smooth.

Add the melted butter and blend for 10 more seconds.

Pour over the base and freeze overnight.

Before serving, allow to defrost and top with my jam.

PREP TIME 10 mins
FREEZER-FRIENDLY Yes
R, RSF, GF, V

MAKES 12-16 SLICES

*It always seems impossible until you measure
and weigh isms then it becomes a joy*

The Big Ass Chocolate Cake

Beetroot Cake

There will be times when you feel like quitting and buying a packet mix sugar shit storm mud cake. But you should not give up so easily.

Ingredients

FOR THE CAKE

170g carrot, grated
170g beetroot, grated
300g activated pepitas
170g desiccated coconut
60g cacao powder
10g psyllium husk
A pinch of salt
30g dried dates
70g currants
100ml maple syrup

FOR THE ICING

200g 80% chocolate, melted
250ml Kara coconut cream
1 tsp vanilla extract
A pinch of salt
100ml #JOY

Method

TO PREPARE THE CAKE

Add the dry ingredients to your food processor and pulse until they turn into a fine crumbly texture.

Add the dates, currants, and maple syrup to the dry mixture and process until well combined.

Transfer the mixture to a round 22cm x 4.5cm springform tin lined with greaseproof paper.

Press down the mixture and spread it evenly.

Keep in the fridge until the icing is ready.

TO PREPARE THE ICING

Add all the ingredients to the food processor and process for about 20 seconds.

Allow the icing to rest for 30 minutes in the fridge to firm up a bit.

Spread the icing over the cake and store the cake in the fridge before serving.

PREP TIME 10-15 mins
FREEZER-FRIENDLY Yes
R, RSF, GF, NF, V

MAKES 12-16 SLICES

Caramel Sauce

Smooth, silky and thick, it's more like a spread than a sauce.

*Because we use coconut cream and coconut sugar it has a unique flavour.
The addition of a little salt makes it explode with flavour.*

Put it on toast, replace jam in the middle of cake, or use your imagination.

*But be patient when you make it. And give it LOTS of love and attention.
Stir it all the time and it won't burn. Instead the flavours will blend to perfection
and turn in to the stuff that dreams are made of.*

Ingredients

250ml Kara coconut cream
60g coconut sugar
A pinch of salt
1/2 tsp vanilla extract,
seeds or paste
10ml #FAITH

Method

Add the coconut cream and sugar to a pot.

Bring to a low simmer and cook for 25 minutes while stirring regularly.

When the mixture gets a caramel consistency, stir in the salt and vanilla.

Transfer to a container and let cool completely before putting the lid on.

Store in the fridge for up to 10 days.

COOKING TIME 30-45 mins
FREEZER-FRIENDLY No
C, GF, RSF, NF, V

SERVES 4-6

Coconut Cherry Rough

These bittersweet, coconutty pockets of joy are raw, easy to make and a real crowd-pleaser when you need something quick.

Throw it into the food processor and then take it from there. The sour cherries complement the sweet chocolate perfectly, and the coconut brings it all home.

Ingredients

40g cacao butter, melted
100ml Kara coconut cream
30g cacao powder
50g coconut sugar
1/2 tsp vanilla extract
30g shredded coconut
A pinch of salt
40g almond butter
100g dried sour cherries
10ml #COMFORT

Method

Add all ingredients to your food processor and blend for 5 seconds to combine the ingredients.

Transfer to a 21.6cm x 11.4cm x 6.35cm tin lined with baking paper.

Press down to distribute evenly and form into a solid base.

Place in the fridge until it firms up.

Cut into small pieces and serve.

PREP TIME 5 mins
FREEZER-FRIENDLY Yes
R, RSF, GF, V

MAKES 25 BITE-SIZE PIECES

RICH—able to celebrate and experience your most authentic life.

Banoffee Cheesecake

- RAW -
Banoffee Cheesecake

OK OK - listen up everyone. This dessert comes with a WARNING.

This pie is NOT to be served like your standard BIG ass slice of pie... HELL no!

Cut it into 16-18 slices or more. Why? The ingredients are dense and filled with nutrients - or in other words: it's fricken decadent all day long.

I sent samples of this dessert to my mate Rachelle's house while she and some friends were doing a business hackathon. Let's just say we know how to mix work and pleasure.

Her whole team responded with video messages of them scoffing my desserts in between bouts of copywriting and design.

This cake is Rachelle's favourite (besides the pavlova, which has an eternal place in her hall of fame). But naming rights go to Hayley who said in her video message "we're going to call this Banoffee Cheesecake, Chef – that's the name!"

Ladies and Gents, I present to you the Banoffee Cheesecake.

You have been warned.

Ingredients

FOR THE BASE

65g sunflower seeds

145g shredded coconut

35g black sesame seeds

20g white tahini

125g dried dates, chopped

40g sultanas

A pinch of salt

45ml water

FOR THE BANANA CARAMEL

200g raw cashew nuts, soaked overnight

200g fresh bananas, chopped

120ml coconut oil, melted

45g coconut sugar

2 tsp vanilla extract

A pinch of salt

150g of my Banana Candy

FOR THE COCONUT CUSTARD

200g raw cashew nuts, soaked overnight

250ml Kara coconut cream

120ml maple syrup

1 tsp lemon juice

A pinch of salt

120ml coconut oil, melted

100g #LETTINGGO

Method

TO PREPARE THE BASE

Add all the ingredients except the water to your food processor and pulse for a few seconds until it breaks down.

Gradually pour in the water and keep the food processor running until the ingredients are well combined and have turned into a sticky dough.

Transfer the mixture to a loose-bottom round 23.5cm x 5.5cm tart tin lined with baking paper.

Press to spread the mixture evenly, press down firmly and set aside.*

TO PREPARE THE BANANA CARAMEL

Add all the ingredients, except the cocout oil, to the blender and blend until smooth. Reduce the speed to low and slowly add the coconut oil. Blend for a few second until well combined.

Pour over the custard and keep the cheesecake in the freezer to set.

Transfer to the fridge to defrost before serving.

*If you have base leftovers, roll them into balls, dip into melted chocolate and serve with afternoon tea.

TO PREPARE THE COCONUT CUSTARD

Add all the ingredients, except for the coconut oil, into the blender and blend until creamy and reduce the speed to low and slowly add the coconut oil. Blend for a few second until well combined.

Pour the custard over the base and keep in the freezer to firm up.

PREP TIME 10 mins

FREEZER-FRIENDLY Yes

R, RSF, GF, V

MAKES 16-18 SLICES

Look what an avocado can do
Avo Chocolate Torte

Avo Chocolate Torte

This is a winner when you want something fast but decadent.
Word up that this beauty will have a mousse-like consistency if you leave it out.
Personally I prefer it firm, but go with your heart.

Speaking of which, the decoration on top is the part that will open your heart
into an enormous smile. People eat with their eyes, not just their mouths,
so watch their faces when you serve up this glorious creation.
Post a pic and tag me on social media so I can be a part of that smile too.

And really: how great is life when we get to make yummy chocolate situations like
this that are actually nourishing and GOOD for our health? Yum!

Ingredients

FOR THE CAKE BASE

145g roasted hazelnuts
45g shredded coconut
120g dried dates
10g cacao powder
15g black tahini
A pinch of salt
Water, as much as needed
(I started off with 15ml)

FOR THE FILLING

2 avocados
100ml Kara coconut cream
170g cacao paste, melted
75g coconut sugar (you can
use more if you like)
1 tsp vanilla extract
A pinch of salt
Maple syrup, optional
(I added a splash for extra
sweetness)
50g #ABUNDANCE

Method

TO PREPARE THE CAKE BASE

Line a loose-bottom 34.5cm x 11cm x 2.5cm rectangular tart tin lined with baking paper, set aside.

Add the ingredients to your food processor and process until combined and the mixture becomes sticky.

If needed, add a 15 mls of water at a time to make the ingredients come together.

Transfer to the prepared tin, press and spread evenly.

TO PREPARE THE FILLING

Add the ingredients except for the maple syrup to your food processor and process until smooth and combined.

Taste and add maple syrup if you want it sweeter.

Flood the cake base with the filling, spread evenly and keep in the freezer to set.

PREP TIME 10 mins
FREEZER-FRIENDLY Yes
R, RSF, GF, V

MAKES 10-12 SLICES

Granola Cookies

Granola cookies. Simple. Profound. Delicious. Nourishing.

Add a little dribble of melted chocolate and they become dangerously addictive.

I have to say these cookies are the best damn situation I've made in a long time.

Just mind the chocolate dribble ok. My friends nearly came to blows fighting over which cookie had the most chocolate dribble.

Like I said. Addictive.

Ingredients

FOR THE BASE

100g coconut flour
115g peanut butter
120ml maple syrup
1/2 tsp vanilla extract
1 tsp cinnamon powder
A pinch of salt
85g vegan dark chocolate
85g vegan white chocolate
75g pumpkin seeds
60g sunflower seeds
140g raisins
115g oats
45g coconut flakes
1/4 cup tahini
10ml #FORGIVENESS

FOR THE TOPPINGS

50g vegan dark chocolate, melted
50g vegan white chocolate, melted

Method

Add all the base ingredients to your food processor and blend for 10 seconds to combine the ingredients. Don't overmix as the mixture needs to have some texture but still be sticky enough.

Divide the mixture into 40g pieces, squeeze the balls until they firm up and then mould each ball into a cookie shape.

Arrange the cookies on a large tray lined with baking paper, drizzle them with the melted chocolate and keep in the fridge to set.

PREP TIME 15mins
FREEZER-FRIENDLY Yes
R, RSF, V

MAKES 20 COOKIES

Lemon Polenta Cake

Lemon Polenta Cake

*When these little puppies came out of the oven
I knew in that very moment each cake needed some extra love.*

*I quickly mixed lemon juice and maple syrup to get a wonderful
balance of sweet with sour and poured it over the hot cakes.*

O M G. My taste buds lit up and my heart exploded.

*We ate them warm right then and there with a big dollop of coconut yoghurt.
This is what #contentment tastes like.*

*Store them in the fridge and if you notice they get a little dry
just heat them gently before serving again.*

Ingredients

FOR THE CAKE

20g chia seeds, ground
100g fine polenta
80g Bob's Red Mill
Gluten Free All-Purpose
Baking Flour
1 tsp baking powder
30g shredded coconut
30g almond meal
A pinch of salt
100g coconut butter,
melted
50ml coconut oil
200ml maple syrup
100ml lemon juice
100ml Kara coconut cream
5 lemon slices
10ml #JOY

FOR THE SYRUP

60ml lemon juice
30ml maple syrup

Method

Preheat your oven at 160C / 320F.

Grease 5 ramekins with coconut oil and line the bottom of each with baking paper.

Arrange the ramekins on a baking tray and set aside.

Combine all the dry ingredients.

In a separate bowl, whisk together all the wet ingredients.

Gradually add the wet mixture to the dry and mix until well combined.

Place a slice of lemon into each ramekin and fill with the batter 1cm before the top.

Bake in the preheated oven for about 35 minutes.

Whisk together the lemon juice and maple syrup and as soon as the cakes are out of the oven, pour the syrup over each cake and leave them to cool completely.

Run a knife around the cakes, tip them over onto a plate and serve.

PREP TIME 5 mins
BAKING TIME 35 mins
FREEZER-FRIENDLY No
C, RSF, GF, V

MAKES 5 CAKES

Wanna Be Brownie

This name comes from my friend Daina, who apparently turned into a brownie expert all of a sudden as she sat on my bed critiquing this recipe.

"Needs more salt..."

Oh, really?

"The sweet potatoes would be much sweeter if we were in New Zealand".

Um, ok.

"It would be much better if I could have some of that crack chocolate spread to smear on it".

Right-o - here you go.

"OK that right there, that's the bomb. Don't change a thing!"

This Wannabe Brownie is rich with flavours of sweet potato, cacao, maple and oats. Smear some of my crack chocolate spread on it and it only gets better.

Ingredients

500g sweet potato, peeled, chopped and steamed
50g cacao powder
100g oat flour
120ml maple syrup
50ml coconut oil
A pinch of salt
150g vegan white chocolate, cut into chunks
150g vegan 80% dark chocolate, cut into chunks
4 dried dates, soaked in 100ml hot water for 10 minutes (reserve 30ml of soaking water)
A pinch of #ABUNDANCE

Method

Preheat your oven to 150C / 302F.

Line a 20cm x 20cm slice tray with baking paper and set aside.

Add the cooled sweet potato to your food processor and process until soft.

Add the cacao powder and oat flour and process for 15 more seconds.

Add the remaining ingredients including the 30ml reserved soaking water and blend for 10 more seconds.

Transfer to the prepared tray and bake for 35-40 minutes.

Leave to cool completely before serving.

PREP TIME 10 mins
BAKING TIME 35-40 mins
FREEZER-FRIENDLY Yes
C, RSF, NF, V

MAKES 15-18 SLICES

Sweet Spiced Milk

This aromatic, hot and sweet milk also features in my first book, Plant-based Love Stories. It is quick to make with no fuss at all and is my go-to sweet drink that makes out like a little hug when there's no one else around. I'll brew up some spiced milk, curl up on the couch, snuggle into my blanket and sink into the love I have for my body and the gratitude I have for the life I've led so far.

I sip away, close my eyes and fall into the NOW as I hold myself knowing that I'm never alone. I have myself, and I'm so worth taking care of.

You'll feel the same when you take your time to brew this special concoction and sip it lovingly.

Ingredients

2 cardamom pods
1/2 tsp vanilla seeds
1 clove
2-3 dates, pitted
550ml coconut milk
A pinch of salt
1 cinnamon stick
1 tbsp #CARE

Method

Add everything except the cinnamon stick to a blender and blend until well combined.

Transfer to a pot, add the cinnamon stick and cook on low (don't allow the milk to boil).

When your spiced milk is hot enough, transfer to a cup and serve.

PREP TIME 1 min
COOKING TIME 5-8 mins
FREEZER-FRIENDLY No
C, RSF, NF

MAKES 550 ML

goooooorgeous
French Toast

French Toast

*Picture this - I was in my studio getting ready to film another recipe
when one of the cameramen asked: What are we making today?
I was like sh*t, not sure. We had a quick scan around the kitchen and
decided to give the classic French toast a crack. Innovative: yes. Classic: no!*

We looked at each other and I remember thinking: Hope this works.

And boy did it work! It was magnificent!

*Here's a tip: watch the heat on this recipe as the almond meal tends to burn.
Cook it slowly and adjust the heat up and down to get it a bit crispy around the edges.
The toppings that I use are essential as they make everything come together
in a truly tasty, epic way.*

*Report back on my social media with your pics and thoughts
on this sweet, yummy goodness.*

Ingredients

FOR THE TOAST

1 cup coconut milk or any other plant-based milk
1/2 tsp vanilla extract
1/4 tsp cinnamon powder
1/2 tsp allspice
2 tbsp almond meal
4 slices sourdough or gluten-free bread
A pinch of salt
Coconut oil, for frying

FOR THE TOPPINGS

Loads of berries and shower with maple syrup and coconut yogurt
A pinch of #INSPIRATION

Method

Heat a pan on medium-low.

Whisk together the milk, vanilla and spices and let it steep for 5 minutes.

Strain and stir in the almond meal.

Add the bread slices (one at a time) to the infused milk and allow them to soak the liquid.

Add a splash of coconut oil to a pan on low heat and cook the bread slices until golden brown and crispy around the edges on both sides.

Top with the blueberries and raspberries.

Sprinkle with cacao nibs, drizzle with coconut yogurt and maple syrup and enjoy!

PREP TIME 5 mins
COOKING TIME 10-15 mins
FREEZER-FRIENDLY No
C, RSF, V

SERVES 4

Sticky Date Pudding

Flashtags

A flash in the oven, so what are these #Flashtag?

"Hey Cynthia, I have a question for you, in The Big Ass Chocolate Cake, what is one cup of #grateful? Is it a brand? Where can I buy that?"

Ask Kat Dawes...

The ingredient you are seeing is not a hashtag, it's a 'flashtag'. It is an invitation for you to feel something – to connect a little deeper with yourself. As you assemble your beautiful ingredients and start to follow the cooking processes, remember your #vibe IS an ingredient, your #energy IS going into the food. What are you feeling?

Just like being mindful of a sharp knife, your energy is a tool and you want to use it very wisely. After all, isn't food that is made with #love noticeably more tasty? And aren't you more likely to burn the bread when you are #frustrated? Behind every thing we do there is thought, and behind every thought there is a feeling (#). When you get down to it, it is #vibes that fuel our lives. The energy of what we are BEing in the present moment – flavours our life's story.

In the world of NOWism, there is much focus brought to the importance of energy, emotion, vibration and feeling, and it is highlighted by marking it with a (#). It's not a hashtag, it's a flashtag! It's the vibe that you are BEing while you are living life. Where are YOU #flashing in from?

Kat Dawes, NOWism.

My spiritual teacher and BFFFFFFFFFFFFF

#JOY -

#joy is found in the sweet side of life! Like the beaming energy of the sun in spring; luminous and bright it erupts from inside into a smile. "My life is sweet!"

#EASE & FLOW

Like liquid gold flowing from a silver spoon, nothing is sweeter than watching the ease and flow of a spoon of honey. No hindrances, or delays, just an elegant stream of precious, sweet energy and momentum. "I am always in the right place at the right time."

#LETTINGGO

We let go to make room for more sweetness. Trusting that that which is no longer needed gently falls away to make room for something greater. Letting go is the art of the great surrender! "I love letting go!"

#COMFORT

A waft of baked delight coming from the kitchen. A sense of softness, security and sweetness. Home sweet home. "I am exactly where I should be, at this moment NOW!"

#GRATITUDE

A sense of fullness, a realisation of the treasure that is your life! Gratitude is the realisation, the gift has already been given. Let us count the ways! "I am so grateful for the abundance of sweetness in my life!"

#FORGIVENESS -

Forgiveness is #freedom in disguise. A courageous decision to be a broadcast of #love. To volunteer to clean up the spilt oak milk! As I #forgive I generate my own sense of #freedom.

#FAITH

I may not know what I am doing but I find out what I need to know when I need to know it. "I can safely take the leap because the universe has my back."

#LOVE -

The chia seed of the cosmos, holding all of reality together, "#love is what I am made of, #love is what I bring."

#COURAGE

Like a fast flame of high heat, it takes courage to go all in. But what is more rewarding than when you bring that wild burn down to a controlled sizzle? Courage is the leap I take when I understand that readiness is over-rated. What I want – wants me! Not ready and going all in. (fist pump).

#PEACE

Hands wrapped around a humble mug of chai. Behind all the busyness there is a clear field – it is always present and peaceful. "All my needs are met!"

#RESPECT

A deeper dive into the moment. A moment of connection. Marvel at the maple tree that brought you the divine syrup which sweetened your Apple pie. "As I look deeper I uncover the blessings!"

#POSITIVITY

Positivity is celebration of the perfection of life! "My positive focus is an alkaline focus – it supports me in endless ways."

#ACCEPTANCE

Acceptance is the art of falling in love with where you are. "I can grow very powerfully from where I am planted!"

#PATIENCE

Usually found on the bottom shelf, #patience is a distant cousin of #trust. There is an art to letting things unfold in their own timing. "I trust in the divine timing of my life! I am at ease while I wait."

#TRUST

It's a big vibe! Very handy when it comes to baking. It can cost you an entire dish if you don't have some handy in the kitchen! "Trust is knowing that I find out what I need to know – when I need to know it!"

#ABUNDANCE

Not just for the decadent moments in life. Abundance is sneaky! It is everywhere! "As I train my eyes to see the availability around me - I never go without! Grateful for this overflow and abundance in my life!"

#INSPIRATION

Like an avocado whipped into an altered state of creamy #bliss! A surprising and delightful vibration that can create worlds! "I am surrounded by so many blessings! It is easy to be inspired!"

#CONTENTMENT

Soft. Safe. Yummy. Sweet. Contentment is knowing that you are exactly where you should be in this moment in time. "Happy right where I am, and also eager for more."

#SELFWORTH

The longest and most delicious romance of your life. Your relationship with you. "I was born worthy! My worth is based on my existence – not my achievements!"

#CARE

Care is #love smeared into an action. "As I express care, I am in a high quality, conscious participation with this moment."

One ingredient and a pinch of salt

Peanut Butter

In the Pantry

I only have one criteria for my ingredients which makes it really easy.

All my ingredients are biodynamic or organic.

Organic food is farmed without synthetic chemicals, growth promoters, hormones or genetically modified components. It's better for the soil, better for the planet and better for you.

Biodynamic food is even better. It's organic food which is holistically cultivated according to a set of natural principles to replenish the soil and create a sustainable enterprise.

If it so happens that I can't find biodynamic or organic food then I don't panic either. I'd rather stress less, make do with what's available and look a bit harder next time.

HERE'S WHAT YOU'LL FIND IN MY PANTRY.

FLOURS

White Spelt

White spelt is a stunning flour with an incredible depth in flavour. It feels good in my body, too. I prefer and always look for biodynamic spelt flour when handing over my hard earned cash.

Bob's Red Mill Gluten Free All-Purpose Baking Flour

I have loved Bob's Red Mill products for over 20 years, and I have also watched them expand while sharing their wealth with their employees. I use the Gluten Free All Purpose Flour only when baking gluten free recipes, and it's wonderful. Their gluten free mix is made with garbanzo bean flour, potato starch, whole grain white sorghum flour, tapioca flour and fava bean flour.

Almond Meal (ground almonds)

Whenever I can, I make my own almond meal by grinding raw almonds in a food processor.

Coconut Flour

Bob's Red Mill Organic Coconut Flour is delicious and nutritious, created from the highest quality desiccated coconut. Their coconut flour is sulphur free.

Corn flour

Corn flour is an extremely versatile flour milled from dried whole corn kernels. I am after the GMO free cornflour.

Oat Flour

Oat flour is milled from oats. You can do it yourself by simply adding oats to your food processor or blender, and blend them down to a flour.

Besan or chickpea flour

Chickpea flour is made from dried chickpeas also known as garbanzo beans, and has a distinct earthy, nutty taste.

Buckwheat flour

Buckwheat flour has a sweet aroma with an earthy, nutty and intense flavour. It can also easily be made. Whenever I have buckwheat kernels, I grind them and make my own buckwheat flour.

DRIED FRUITS

Currants

Zante currants or simply currants are dried, seedless red grapes with a sweet and tangy taste.

Raisins

Raisins are simply dried grapes – they are allowed to dry and shrivel up for around three weeks. A range grape varieties are used to make them, and the size, taste, and colour depend on the type of grape used.

Golden Raisins

Golden raisins are plump, soft, and fruitier. You may have also heard the term sultana. In the US, this sweet treat is called golden raisins or sultana raisins. In the UK, Australia, and other places they are called simply sultanas.

Sour Cherries

They are also called tart cherries. Dried, organic sour cherries are a dark colour when dried.

Fig

It is a vibrant fruit that works with sweet and savoury dishes, they are also great to bake with.

Goji Berries

Known for their sweet, slightly sour flavor and vibrant red hue. It is a must that your choose ones without sulphur and oil.

Dates

I used organic dried dates.

FRUITS AND BERRIES

Strawberries

Use organic, frozen and fresh.

Blackberries

Use organic, frozen and fresh.

Blueberries

Use organic, frozen and fresh.

Raspberries

Use organic, frozen and fresh.

Banana

Use the Cavendish variety.

Apple

There are so many varieties of apples out there. I suggest you use the Granny Smith apple to do any baking or cooking. It has less water content – that's what Dee said.

Lemon

Use fresh, organic, juicy lemons.

Orange

Use organic Navel oranges.

Mango

Use mangoes that are ripe as possible (if you are using frozen chunks, make sure they are well thawed before using them in baking).

Avocado

Use the Hass variety.

Cherries

Use fresh, organic, and juicy cherries.

Passion Fruit

Using fresh passion fruit is the best. I love the little purple variety that has so much flavour. Sweet and sour, all in one incredible fruit.

Pineapple

Use pineapples that are ripe as possible (if you are using frozen chunks, make sure they are well thawed before using them in baking).

Dragon fruit

Use dragon fruits that are ripe as possible.

Lime

Use fresh, organic, juicy limes.

Figs

Use ripe fresh figs.

SPICES

Cinnamon powder

Did you know it's super easy to make your own cinnamon powder? Break up cinnamon bark into chunks, blend them using a high-speed blender, pass them through a sieve, and voilà – fresh cinnamon powder.

Turmeric powder

Organic dried turmeric is powerful in flavour so be mindful.

Vanilla pods

Use long, fresh, semi-dried pods. I use the seeds together with the pod by cutting it into 1 inch slices and either chucking them into the blender, or popping them into a cooked desert as is.

Vanilla extract

I prefer to use the sugar-free one.

All Spice

Allspice is a spice made from the dried berries of a plant known as Pimenta dioica.

Nutmeg

I used whole nutmeg and used a microplane grater to turn it into powder.

Cardamom Seeds

Use the green pods.

Ginger

Use fresh organic, unpeeled, grated ginger.

SWEETENERS

Coconut sugar

I use a very good coconut sugar made in Indonesia. Make sure that you choose a pure one, with as little human interference as possible.

Maple syrup

I use pure maple syrup and I love it. It's gorgeous!

Raw Sugar

Raw sugars are produced directly from the cane juice in a sugar mill close to cane fields.

After the juice is extracted and clarified, it undergoes a single-crystallization process. Crystals are then centrifuged to remove most of the cane molasses.

VINEGAR

Apple cider vinegar

My brand of choice is Braggs. They have an amazing organic apple cider vinegar which contains the "mother" – a combination of yeast, proteins and friendly bacteria which form during the fermentation process.

CACAO PRODUCTS

I always choose organic products from Fairtrade.

The seeds of life

Cacao powder

I used organic Indonesian and Peruvian cacao powder.

Cacao paste

I used organic Indonesian and Peruvian cacao paste.

Cacao nibs

I used organic Indonesian and Peruvian cacao nibs.

Cacao butter

I used organic Indonesian and Peruvian cacao butter.

CHOCOLATE

White Chocolate

I use organic white chocolate sweetened with coconut sugar.

70% Dark Chocolate

I use 70% organic dark chocolate sweetened with coconut sugar.

80% Dark Chocolate

I use 80% organic dark chocolate sweetened with coconut sugar.

SEEDS, NUTS, GRAINS

Chia

This will come as no shock, but chia seeds (ground down) are an important staple for almost any plant-based baking recipe. They are a fantastic binding agent (and they're great for your gut)! Chia seeds are one of the richest plant source of omega-3 fatty acids.

Psyllium Husk

Or powder.

Raw Cashews

I used raw and organic cashews. I roast them when needed to make a nut butter.

Raw flax seeds

Flax seeds are full of fibre, and the richest plant source of omega-3 fatty acids.

Raw hemp seeds

Delicious raw, hulled or unhulled organic hemp hearts.

Raw pecans

Americans are divided over the pronunciation of this nut, with roughly half preferring PEE-can and the other half saying pe-KAWN.

Raw pumpkin seeds

Called "Pepitas" in Spanish, or as I know them, pumpkin seeds. They are green and tasty.

Raw Quinoa

Pronounced KEEN-wah, this ancient grain is actually a seed and is packed with nutrition. Freezes well after cooked.

Raw Sunflower Seeds

Organic seeds are the best.

Raw Hazelnuts

I use raw and activated hazelnuts. I roast the raw ones when making nut butters.

Raw Almonds

I use raw and activated almonds. I roast the raw ones when making nut butters.

Raw Walnuts

I used whole shelled and organic walnuts.

Raw Sesame Seeds White and Black

Toasting brings out the nutty flavour in these flat, tear-shaped seeds. Black or white, these seeds are legends.

Roasted Almond Butter

Organic.

Roasted peanut butter

Organic.

White glutinous rice

Organic.

Black Glutinous Rice

Organic.

Polenta

a.k.a. Corn Grits.

Dehydrated Whole Buckwheat Groats

Organic.

Oats

Use organic pressed oats.

OIL

Cold-pressed olive oil

Organic.

Cold-pressed, non-deodorised, unfiltered coconut oil

Organic.

Rice Bran Oil

Organic.

MILK

Any plant-based milk e.g. oat milk, almond milk, soy milk

Look for milk that's as pure as possible. I encourage you to make milk on your own but if you choose to buy, check the label and opt for one with ingredients as close to nature as possible. Also, the less sugar, oil and numbers the better!

COCONUT PRODUCTS

Coconut cream

The brand I truly trust is Kara.

Cultured coconut yogurt

Buy the purest one you can find.

Desiccated coconut

The best one is without any sulphur. Bob's Red Mill is the brand I recommend.

Coconut flakes

As with desiccated coconut, the best product out there is the one without sulphur. I like Bob's Red Mill products.

Coconut Butter

I made my own (check the recipe under coconut butter).

Coconut Powder

Use dehydrated coconut milk powder that you can later add water to, and turn back into coconut milk.

BITS AND PIECES

Baking powder

My preferred brand is Bob's Red Mill.

Baking Soda

My preferred brand is Bob's Red Mill.

Dried Yeast

I used active baker's yeast that's dried. It's an active yeast when used in baking.

Savoury yeast

The organic kind (sometimes referred to as nutritional yeast), it's an inactive yeast.

Water

#BLESSED

Chickpea Water

A can of chickpeas (the water only).

Beetroot

Fresh bright red beets.

Sweet Potato

Any kind of fresh sweet potato, as long as they are sweet.

Pumpkin

Butternut or Kent pumpkin is what I love, as they are sweet. The sweeter the better.

YL Oil (Young Living Oil)

Young Living is the choice of essential oils I love to use. If you're keen to use them let me know and I will send you the details.

Love Yes love, the kind you find within

#LOVE

Tahini, Black and White

Black tahini is from black sesame seeds, and white tahini is from white sesame seeds, grounded down to make a paste called tahini.

Silken Tofu

There are so many different brands out there, I used a GMO free organic brand.

Wild Medicine Flower Essences

I used a Butterscotch flavour for the Sticky Date pudding.

Bread Crumbs

Use your choice of gluten free bread – slice, then toast, and then process in the food processor.

Brandy

Booze LOL...

The stuff my grandmother used to soak dried fruit in to make her fruit cake for Christmas.

Butterfly Pea Powder

A bright blue flour that is so damn special. Dried then turned into a powder, makes a fantastic blue dye colour.

Nut Butter

I am the world's bestest nut butter maker ever. I roast the organic nuts, blend them, add a pinch of salt – DONE. Peanut Butter and Almond Butter are my choice. Brand-wise, well, biodynamic or organic roasted nut butters are the best.

Egg Replacement

Bob's Red Mill is a great brand that I have used throughout this book. Gluten Free Vegan Egg Replacer is simple, clean, and easy-to-use.

Salt

Choose unrefined salt and don't be afraid to experiment! There is a whole chapter on Salt in my first book Plant-Based Love Stories. Salt is an incredible flavour enhancer, and it pairs with chocolate like you wouldn't believe. Try sea salt, Himalayan salt, Celtic sea salt or Maldon salt flakes. Just avoid refined table salt.

Strawberry Coconut Cream Pie

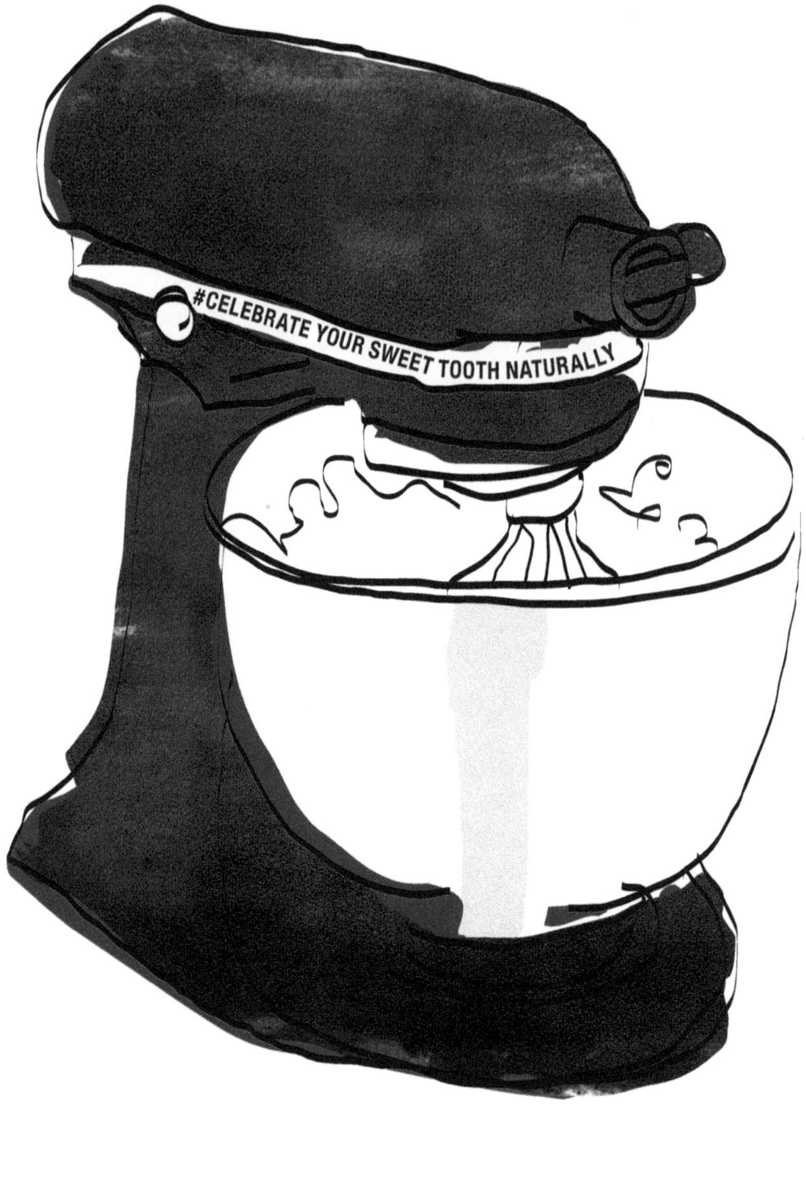
#CELEBRATE YOUR SWEET TOOTH NATURALLY

Equipment

Scales
(1g) scales

Measuring (1L) Jug

Measuring spoons (ml)

Vitamix
high speed blender

Food processor
any one will do

Kitchenaide
comes with dough hook, whisk
and paddle

Oven (fan forced)
I have a gas oven and it gets HOT!

Knife
Japanese

Cutting board
hardwood

Tart tin

Round Springform Tin

Square Baking Tray

Rectangle Baking Tray

Large Cup Cake Tray

Small Cupcake Tray

Large Cupcake Paper Cases
unbleached

Small Cupcake Paper Cases
unbleached

Magnum Ice Cream Molds
blocks of 4

Ice Block Molds
blocks of 6-8

Baking Trays

Baking Paper
unbleached

Ice Cream Scoop

Spatula
large off-set spatula

Stainless Steel Bowls
all sizes

Kitchen tweezers

Rolling Pin
60cm long

Dehydrator
I used my 9-tray Excalibur dehydrator
but any dehydrator will do the job

All I can say is - Thanks!

Acknowledgements

Mum & Dad. Thank you for introducing me to Christmas fruit cake. It wasn't till I was older that I really understood your connection with it. Now, it's one of my favourite sweets.

I love you both.

Jayman. I know you will love these recipes. One day when you're ready and have your own children this book will be a legacy for you and your future family. I can't thank you enough for all the years you spat out anything tahini, or wrinkled your nose at the smell before you got into the kitchen.

I am a better chef because of your constant criticism and commitment to sweets.

I love you dearly.

Courtney. I celebrate the love we both have for great food. Your positive vibe has been a lifesaver.

Your countless private messages have had me laughing so hard my belly hurts.

Thank you for being such a dear friend to me.

I love you.

Gungun. You have outdone yourself this time, not just with the camera but with every mouthful of sweets you ate after each shoot. We know it was you who ate the chocolate!

Thank you for your care and calmness during the many hours we spent shooting these recipes.

You remain my guru of #ease.

Russ. The Great Writer Man. If I could only find the words that would describe how incredible it is to have you in my life on the phone, away for weekends, at dinner on Fridays, or those mid-week sneaky dinner parties at yours, or on my couch.

Your brain is outstanding.

You're fast, smart and super gentle when it comes to taking my many words and sentences and making them better.

Much much better :).

You have had me in tears with your words and I have had you in laughter with mine.

I love you!

Dee. Look at you go. Correcting, reading, and more correcting. Making sure I am on-point and making sure I am focused when creating on and off the camera.

Thank you for your constant care and love of my sweet recipes.

Rachelle. When you find a sweet you love you go all in. Like the banoffee pie. You claimed that one and pretty much ate half of it. You crack me up. I love it when I make a gluten-free sweet situation and you either love it or turn up your lip and flair your nose. A clear sign it's not good enough.

Thanks for being so honest. And thanks for being my dear friend.

I love you.

Daina. You are a real sweet tooth. One I can solidly count on. You have quietly (not like my other mates) chewed away slowly and sank into the sweetness of each recipe you tasted.

Then, and only then would you quietly comment.

Thanks mate for being that person.

FYI, sorry I have ruined all your sweet adventures outside of my kitchen. The disappointment in your eyes when you eat a sweet something out there in the real world is priceless!!

I loved having you in this space with me. Thanks mate! x

My Mates. To all my mates who came to the studio with your Tupperware containers, thank you for your mouths and tummies. I loved watching you fall in love with my sweet recipes while we chatted, laughed, argued, and did it all again. My recipes are better because of you.

Jon Gwyther. What a privilege it is to have you in my life. Your ability to catch the right light that brings out the truth in my face is nothing short of genius. You kindly and willingly fitted in my shoot just two days before you decided to walk (solo) around the island of Bali (who the hell does that??). Thank you from my heart to yours for taking that time to catch me once again. I love you.

My spiritual Teacher and Coach. Kat Dawes, not only am I a better human from your coaching over the last 10 years, I am a more present human. For that, I feel that every single person must make their way to you.

Thank you.

I love you (and not the red lollie kind either!)

Kymba. I can't thank you enough as you created the design and layout of my first cookbook Plant-based Love Stories – and here is my second one! Your creative mind and design genius is so heartfelt it's no wonder your company is called Soulful Branding.

My Team of Wonderful Humans. Your care and love of my work makes my heart sing. Life is certainly better with you all in it. Thank you for being my rock and my caretaker as I navigate the ever changing online world and the physical world.

The Farmers of Indonesia. I can't thank you enough for your sweet coconut sugar, edible flowers of apple blossom, and wild amaranth.

I am in deep gratitude for the constant flow of fresh cacao, vanilla, cinnamon and the many tropical fruits I have the pleasure of eating. Your deep care of the soil, the water, and the deep spirit of this land is an honour to connect with.

Christina. Every single person should have the pleasure of finding you and your jewellery that I am always wearing. Thank you for your endless care, support and love. It's not only how beautiful your pieces are, it is more about what you represent – that is the true gold.

Simone. You would have to be my one friend that loves chocolate more than I do, You make me laugh so much when ever we eat out, you say to me just order all the chocolate desserts mate, like all of them!! righto mate and I do. Love you long time x

Seaenah. I bet you 100 bucks you will always remember me for my cookies. You just love them. It has been 10 years now that I have solidly made your birthday cakes and I am so pleased you love to celebrate your sweet tooth naturally.

To you the reader. Hi and Thank you... Thank you for choosing to Celebrate Your Sweet Tooth Naturally.

Each sweet recipe in this book has your health, your happiness, your organs, and your orgasms in mind.

When we use ingredients that are as close to nature as possible – exactly like the ones I used in these recipes – we come to a realisation: nature gets it right every time!

Something shifts in us. We start to cultivate, internally, a deep value for our bodies and we fall deeply in love with ourselves.

When nature dictates the menu, we are in alignment.

And I promise you this – you will never feel like you are going without.

I created these recipes from the love of my family, my friends, and the people I care about.

If you're holding this book in your hands, you're letting me care for you too.

With love

Chef Cynthia Louise xx

About Chef Cynthia Louise

Chef Cynthia Louise talks about food.

Plant-based food that makes you Feel GOOD.

She won't talk diet.

She won't talk macronutrients.

She talks about real food. Just like nature intended.

And one more thing – if it doesn't have flavour it can F-off.

Chef Cynthia comes with a large side of personality. An infectious passion. Not to mention she's also

- the bestselling author of Plant-based Love Stories and 7 other recipe books (including 3 books with biochemist Dr Libby Weaver)

- the star of 2 cooking shows on Gaia TV and FMTV

- the partner of a global chain of restaurants with serial entrepreneur Roger Hamilton

- served hundreds of people on stage and at retreats in Bali with Tyler Tolman

- and created her own range of gut-healing food products and online classes.

She's an exciting and charismatic public speaker touring Australia for the past decade. Thousands of people who live healthy, pain free, abundant lives through her meals say she knows what she's doing – and it works.

In her early days at a health resort she saw the effects of her cooking on chronically ill patients.

Diabetes, stress, chronic fatigue, Crohn's, eczema, cirrhosis, leaky gut, IBS and autoimmune conditions all responded positively – even to the amazement of natural doctors and healers – when she served natural, plant-based meals made from her highest intentions.

She followed these same principles while recovering from her second heart surgery. So she knows the power of her method from the inside out.

As an adopted child raised in New Guinea, Cynthia spent days down the back of her family's workshop with the wives of the workers. They would harvest coconuts and shred them while roasting sweet potatoes over an open fire. In contrast, her nights at home were spent eating rissoles and mash (don't ask what a rissole is if you don't know).

She learnt early on how real food tastes and what it does for your body.

That's when she realized that cooking is a contract with your body. Our health is on loan. You pay it back by nourishing yourself with positive energy and emotions, then starting the simple act of preparing a meal.

It's one of the many simple, yet profound things Chef Cynthia Louise has discovered in her journey. And there's more she wants to share.

Cook with real food. Cook with great energy. Cook with Chef Cynthia Louise.

PLANT-BASED
LOVE STORIES

97
Real food recipes
that make you
feel good

CHEF CYNTHIA LOUISE

Love is a universal feeling

Recipes

Adult Only Decadent Chocolate Cupcakes	40
Almond and Orange Cake	78
Almond Berry Cake	100
Anzac Biscuits	102
Apple Pie	144
Avo Chocolate Torte	242
Banana Bread	192
Banana Candy	76
Banana Choc Chip Muffins	30
Banana Spring Rolls	136
Banoffee Cheesecake	238
Beetroot Cake	230
Black Salted Caramel Cheesecake	84
Black Sticky Rice	128
Blackcurrant and Strawberry Crumble Slice	220
Blue Bounty	50
Breakfast Carrot Cake	92
Cacao	178
Candy Nuts	214
Caramel Sauce	232
Carrot Cake	172
Chef Travis's Compote	90
Cherry and the Ripe	184
Chewy Bars	60
Choc Chip Cookies	94
Chocolate Crackles	148
Chocolate Orange Truffle Tart	106
Chocolate Snaps	54
Chocolate "Crack" Spread	162
Chocolate Truffle Balls	98
Cinnamon Scrolls	124
Coconut Butter	28
Coconut Cherry Rough	234
Dee's Chocolate Mousse	114
Double Choc Chip Cookies	34
Doughnuts	112

French Toast   256

Granola Cookies   244

Hayley's Brownie   82

Homemade Jam   134

Hot Cross Buns   44

Ice Pops   58

Jam Drop Cookies   20

Jayman's Cake   196

Lamington Fingers   168

Lemon Polenta Cake   248

Magnum Icecreams   188

Mango Coconut Muffins   210

Mixed Berry Crumble   46

Muesli Bars   86

Mum's Quick Treat for the Kids   176

My Dad's Fruit Cake   158

My Mum's Fruit Salad   182

Next Level Chocolate   140

Passionfruit Cheesecake   204

Peanut Butter   160

Peanut Butter Slice   200

Pumpkin Pie   166

Rice Crackles   24

Rustic Chocolate Bar   208

Sticky Date Pudding   70

Strawberry Coconut Cream Pie   226

Sweet Potato Fudge   118

Sweet Spiced Milk   252

The Big Ass Chocolate Cake   218

The Original Tahini Balls   52

The Pav   110

Truffle Protein Balls   62

Very Vegan Berry Cheesecake   190

Wanna Be Brownie   250

White Chocolate & Hazelnut Cookies   72

White Chocolate Cake   18

White Chocolate Mousse   152

Continue the Love

For a glorious flow of plant-based recipes, videos, hints,
tips and online classes, follow me on:

@ **chef cynthia louise**   **www.chefcynthialouise.com**

Cover design and layout by Kymba Burrows

Food Photography by Gun Gun Gumilar

Photography and direction by Jon Gwyther

Food styling by Chef Cynthia Louise

Recipes by Chef Cynthia Louise

All props provided by Chef Cynthia Louise studio kitchen

Author Celebrate Your Sweet Tooth Chef Cynthia Louise

© Chef Cynthia Louise 2021

Publisher Let's EAT Food

First printed in 2021

ISBN: 978-0-6450178-3-0

CPSIA information can be obtained
at www.ICGtesting.com
Printed in the USA
LVHW071511130122
708518LV00010B/805